Fishing for the Abundant Life...
a Journey to Faith

R. C. Balfour III

Sentry Press
424 East Call Street
Tallahassee, Florida 32301

Fishing for the Abundant Life

© 2003 by R.C. Balfour III

Library of Congress Control Number: 2004114540

ISBN 1-889574-21-X

Printed by Colson Printing Company, Valdosta, Georgia

"I am the door; if anyone enters through Me, he will be saved, and will go in and out and find pasture. The thief comes only to steal and kill and destroy; I came that they may have life, and have it abundantly."
Jesus speaking in John 10:9,10 NASB

Contents

Part One
Beginnings

Part Two
Discoveries

v

I dedicate this book to my wife, Virginia, who has been my forthright and honest critic as well as my greatest fan— when I happened to turn out something worth reading.

I would also like to include my children, their spouses, and our grandchildren: Bob, Vicki and Lindsay; Virginia; Deborah, Tommy, Thomas and Rachel; David, Linda, Natalie and Stephanie; Charles, Shannon, Drew, Hayes, and Honey. I pray that they all might experience a challenging but rewarding journey to faith.

Acknowledgments

I wish to thank all those special people who took the time to read my manuscript and make constructive suggestions. They include my wife Virginia, Anne King, Tom Perry, my daughter Deborah Crabtree, author William Rogers, retired clergyman Bob Slane, my minister Chuck Bennett and three other clergymen, Charles Fulton, Alan Hansen, and Mike Flynn. I also want to thank my secretary Ann Delaney for her usual "wild goose chases" on the telephone, for her clerical support, and her suggestions. Robert Crawford offered good technical advice. Dave Polstra kept faith in my work and offered encouragement. The Florida Fish and Wildlife Conservation Commission and artist Diane Peebles furnished images of many saltwater fish, which aided artist Bob Dixon with his sketches. I thank John Jauregui and Dan Glaze for their valuable assistance and Wendy Colson for his patience and interest. Forrest (Cutter) Knapp Jr. opened several doors. My illustrator, Bob Dixon, offered good suggestions. And I want to thank all my wonderful fishing pals, who have added so much fun and excitement to my life. Finally, thanks be to God who has given me life, deliverance, meaning, and opportunity and is responsible for any achievements I might have made.

PREFACE

When I reached my seventy-fourth birthday, my wife and I took the big step of buying a computer. Now I understand why so many books are written and why publishers discourage the submission of manuscripts. Computers make it so easy to write that many, many books are written.

In my first book I wrote about an unusual and exotic river, which flows from South Georgia into the Gulf of Mexico. *In Search of the Aucilla* has exceeded my expectations as a book of regional interest. All authors know that even a small success at writing is addictive. Usually the author cannot wait to get back to the computer and try his or her hand again. I am no exception.

Besides our family, which includes five children, their spouses, and eight grandchildren, my other major interests are my continued role in timberland management, fishing, and striving to serve Christ and his church. That's why this book is about fishing and faith, two of my passions that intertwine with somewhat similar characteristics.

The book is very personal and I hope very honest. It is an attempt to explain my Christian journey along with lighter reading about some of my fishing experiences. Whereas the journey is in chronological order, many of the fishing stories are flashbacks, told without any particular time sequence. I hope that my journey will help open the way for others who are seeking answers to some of life's basic questions—answers we all eventually search for with great diligence and even a small amount of anxiety.

R.C. Balfour III

PROLOGUE

There's a fascination about fishing that draws people to it. I can't remember when I wasn't a fisherman. There's also a current that draws people to faith. We are blessed when we happen to fall into that current, because once we give up our individual struggle and swim with it, we are saved.

Somehow, there's a connection between the two. The earliest Christian symbols were the cross and two curved lines representing a fish. Both symbols appear on ancient walls and in the catacombs of Rome. The first four disciples of Jesus were fishermen, who were casting or mending nets when he called them.

The last earthly appearance of Jesus in John's Gospel is on the shore of the Sea of Galilee. Some of the disciples have been fishing all night with no luck. Jesus calls out to them to cast the net on the right side of the boat. The nets are so filled with fish they almost break. He then invites them to breakfast with him on the shore where he has fish and bread cooking on a charcoal fire.

Hope and faith are essential to the fisherman—hope that the day will bring encounters with schools of fish, and faith that his lure will be struck by a fish he cannot see. Hope and faith are indispensable to the Christian journey leading to the abundant life.

Jesus invites us to become fishers of men.

The fact that America is in the midst of a culture war between secular materialism and the Judeo-Christian heritage makes our journey more difficult. The media, which we digest in huge quantities each day, has many road signs luring us into temptations and dead ends.

The abundant life does not consist of acquiring many possessions. Extensive possessions tend to demand all our time, putting us in bondage to them. Rather the abundant life consists of the acquisition and exercising of spiritual attributes such as love, joy, peace, patience, and humility. Also forgiveness, faith, generosity, self-control, and perseverance.[1] These character traits release us from the bonds of the flesh and point us toward eternal life.

In this book I would like to relate some of my fishing adventures. At the same time I would like to tell how I fell into the current of faith and began to swim with it toward the abundant life. I hope and pray that my experience will encourage others to test the water.

[1] Based on Galatians 5:22,23 with author's changes and additions.

Part One

BEGINNINGS...

Both my experience in saltwater fishing and my faith journey had unusual beginnings. The fishing experience was exciting and dangerous, while my faith journey began with a sobering realization. Both had a definite sign without which I might not have made it.

CHAPTER 1

I Got The Blues

My introduction to offshore fishing was a little too adventurous. Two of my pals had found an unbelievable spot to catch bluefish. The location was straight out of Ochlockonee River Bay, Florida, about six miles offshore. It consisted of a shallow area of Ochlockonee Shoal called "the knob" by local fishermen.

At low tide, just as the rise started, this sandy shelf was covered with bluefish. When the water was clear they could be seen darting swiftly across the knob, literally by the dozens. Trolling small yellow dusters with a strip of mullet on the forward hook produced instant strikes and the ensuing hard fight, characteristic of bluefish. Many blues would jump clear of the water adding to the excitement.

My pals, Nat and John, invited me to experience this spectacular adventure and I couldn't resist the offer. It didn't matter that John's boat was only 15 feet long—that he had no life jackets and no anchor—and even that he carried only a nickel sized compass. It also didn't matter that I possessed only a small freshwater reel with no star drag. I remedied that situation by wrapping my thumb in adhesive tape to restrain the reel.

We left Trade Winds Pier early one morning and were on the knob by eight o'clock. We had timed the tide just right. It was just beginning to rise as we trailed our lures on the first pass. Instant hookups with the hard fighting blues ensued. My pals' proper equipment handled theirs well, while I lost mine fumbling with my makeshift outfit. We boated the two blues and made another pass. Another triple, and this time we landed all three.

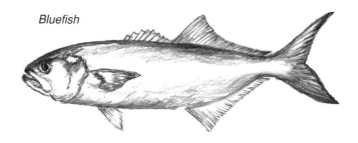
Bluefish

I had been warned about the sharp teeth and the snapping jaws of bluefish. To dispatch the fish quickly into the ice chest, I had been told to grip the blue between my thighs and hold its body tight while extracting the hook. I was amazed at how well this technique worked. Of course, after repeating the trick a few times, our trousers were soaked with fish blood.

We had caught thirty or more fish in a frenzy of activity and were making another pass when I noticed a black cloud forming over the mouth of the Bay. I mentioned it to John, but the remark was lost as the blues struck again with the same fury. Minutes later I glanced back at the cloud, which had now spread across the entire horizon, headed our way.

This time John took notice, but it was a little late. The storm hit us with a ferocity I will never forget. The outboard motor drowned out first, causing our boat to drift sideways at the mercy of the waves, which were approaching five feet with whitecaps. Next, the boat began filling with water and we were soon sitting on the deck, waist deep. Lightning was continually striking the water all around us. John was pretty freaked out, Nat was passively trying to nap, and I was praying as hard as I could.

It soon became apparent that the lapstrake wood boat had reached an equilibrium with the sea and was not going to sink, at least not anytime soon. But another problem became apparent. The wind and seas were steadily blowing us farther offshore. An hour and a half later the storm blew over, leaving us out of the sight of land. John pulled out his ten-cent store compass, but it was full of water immobilizing the needle. Since the sky was overcast and the wind now variable, we had no way of knowing the direction to land.

The cloud had now spread across the entire horizon, headed our way.

Finally, John got the motor dried out and cranked. As the low clouds and mist cleared a little, we all scanned the horizon looking for anything that could give us direction. Then suddenly my eyes came upon it, so small that I had to look twice to be sure. Appearing like a tiny dot on the horizon, it could have easily been missed. It was the tip top of the tallest pine tree on Alligator Point, but it was all we needed. *It was a definite sign pointing us in the right direction*; my prayers had been answered.

Then suddenly my eyes came upon it, so small I had to look twice to be sure.

CHAPTER 2

Getting Pointed in the Right Direction

We must no longer be children, tossed to and fro and blown about by every wind of doctrine.... Ephesians 4:14a NRSV
For the wisdom of this world is foolishness with God.
1st Corinthians 3:19a NRSV

There are a few defining moments in life when the picture becomes clearer. These times leave an indelible impression on us and largely define our character. For me, one of these moments came a few years after I finished college. World War II had ended four years earlier when atomic bombs were dropped on two major Japanese cities.

Passion for the end of the "War to end all wars" coined by Woodrow Wilson during World War I was running high. The United Nations was the child of this wave of optimistic idealism. At that time the idea that man would ascend to a higher plane and solve all problems seemed to prevail.

I had joined a new organization, the World Federalists. Fashioned partly after the *Federalists*, a group of founding fathers who supported the idea of a strong Constitution, this group was pushing for an end to the veto power in the Security Council, thus making UN resolutions binding upon all member states.

After graduating from the University of Georgia, a friend and I made a speaking tour of Southwest Georgia, talking to civic clubs and small groups about the Federalist vision. In one small South Georgia town, we were given a list of community leaders to contact.

All was going our way until we stopped in front of a small neat house, surrounded by beautiful flowers. When we rang the doorbell, an elderly lady opened the door and invited us inside. While enjoying some homemade cookies and lemonade, I gave what I thought was a stirring summary of the Federalist viewpoint. To my astonishment, when I finally wound down, she asked, "Young man, are you aware of what the Bible has to say about all this?"

That wasn't exactly what I wanted to hear, but out of respect for the little old lady, my friend and I listened while she elaborated on the Gospel and the Last Days as described in the Book of Revelation. I concluded that she was just uneducated in the events of the day, provincial and introverted. And what a letdown—she was lecturing *me* about a subject on which I had all the answers. So my friend and I politely dismissed ourselves at the first opportunity, crossed her name off the list, and went looking for people of greater intellect.

Little did I realize that long after all the speeches and excitement about the Federalist movement were forgotten, the words of that lady would still occupy a place in my mind. In fact in time it would be about the only thing I remembered about that summer's adventure. Over fifty years later the same Bible message concerning the Last Days would become the subject of a series of novels, placing high on the nation's best seller's list and read by thousands.

The World Federalist vision was only one of many idealistic views born of that post-war era. Since political science had been my major, much of my required reading concerned the philosophers. The subject of one book was the evolution of the human race. Introduced by Darwin's evolution theory, the book built a thesis on the mental and moral evolution of man. The end of all this would climax in a race of mankind so superior in wisdom and understanding that war, poverty, tyranny, and crime would disappear. The book became widely popular on college campuses among both students and faculty.

These utopian theories found keen reception in the culture of that time, which was still rebounding from the wounds of World War II. Even communism, which in actual practice resulted in a brutal dictatorship, was undergirded by the Marxist theory that in time all elements of government would disappear. People would then live in self-sacrificing and loving communes.

Evolution idealism was popular for several years after the war and began waning only as the Cold War came on. The USSR developed its own atomic bomb and Winston Churchill popularized the expression, Iron Curtain. The quenching of freedom in Hungary and the Cuban missile crisis began to wear away the facade of idealism.

During these years I had immersed myself in building a business and starting a family. My desire to serve others was expressed in civic work, following the example of my father. But I must confess that although much of my civic work bore fruit, some of that effort involved building a reputation for myself.

The shattering of man-centered idealism was the first step in my search for the truth. I concluded that mankind was not evolving at all. The twentieth century was becoming the bloodiest in history. Millions of people were virtually enslaved by totalitarian states. Wars were still breaking out. Human nature had not changed. Crime, underpinned by the drug culture, was as bad or worse than ever. The idea about mankind's evolution just didn't add up. Somewhere in the recesses of my mind, the unheeded words of that little old lady raised a *small but definite sign pointing me in the right direction.*

Part Two

DISCOVERIES...

As we make our way through life, discoveries make our journey colorful and lead us toward the truth. Fishing discoveries make the sport more exciting and productive, while faith discoveries make our lives more meaningful, purposeful and abundant.

Duster (lure) with a strip of bait attached to forward hook.

CHAPTER 3

A New Experience—
Large Wakes Chase Flying Fish

There are a few fishing trips that remain indelibly impressed on my mind. They are the ones when I experienced something *new and unusual.* Such an event happened years ago before I gave up offshore fishing.

One of my regular fishing pals, Shelly Chastain, and I planned an offshore trip for one of our Saturday excursions. Shelly at that time was my regular first mate before he acquired a boat of his own. Shelly's son-in-law rounded out our crew. We were always hunting new bottom fishing spots, which were expressed in loran coordinates. Today satellite instruments called Global Positioning System or GPS have largely replaced loran, but in those days loran was almost too good to be true. It worked by receiving radio signals from two or more radio transmitters located on the shore. The point where these transmissions intersected located any position in the Gulf. A black box called loran interpreted the signals for us.

All boat captains kept a book of loran numbers that designated good bottom formations attractive to large fish. It was a normal practice for captains to swap loran numbers or use any honorable or dishonorable method of extracting numbers from the book of a competitor. I had just made such a swap (honorably) and obtained some new numbers.

We were anxious to try these new locations, and the day brought us beautiful weather, 5 to 10 miles per hour southwest wind with no clouds in the sky. Well, we set out in my 22 foot North American

In the water behind the escaping fish a large wake followed.

till we were about 25 miles offshore. On such perfect days the Gulf of Mexico always displays the same beautiful sights. Its color is light green for about 20 miles. It then changes abruptly to dazzling blue with flying fish streaking away from the boat. When we no longer saw flying fish, we knew we were in the vicinity of good rock holes.

Unfortunately for us, the numbers turned out to be bogus, and our extensive hunt failed to produce fish. That's a forlorn feeling— when you explore a dozen loran readings with an empty fish box. We finally gave up and headed back toward shore.

As we entered the flying fish zone, I was watching these fascinating creatures pick up and fly away when something unusual caught my eye. Fifty yards off our port side I noticed a school of 6 or more flying fish pick up together and glide away. In the water behind the escaping fish a large wake followed. This act repeated itself several times. The wakes following the fish had to be large predators intent upon making a sumptuous meal out of the airborne critters.

I stopped the boat and showed this sight to my crew, who had begun to nap as we began our long ride in. We all got excited and began searching for trolling lures. The only tackle we had on board was heavy bottom rods and reels, not ideal for trolling. Finally we found three large dusters and attached a strip of bait to the forward hooks.

I cranked the motors and trailing our lures, we headed into the midst of the action. I cut ahead of a large wake and moments later one rod doubled with the reel screaming. After securing the other two lines, one of my pals settled down into a vigorous battle with the large fish. Ten minutes later he pulled a monstrous fish to the boat.

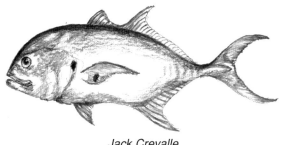

Jack Crevalle

Silver and yellow colors and a large spot on the gills identified a jack crevalle, which is a great gamester, but poor table fare.

A little disappointed, we released the large fish and wondered if any species worth boating was involved in the fray. Just to make sure, we took another swing into the thick of the action. This time my lure was taken and I found myself engaged in a brutal fight—not certain which end of the line would prevail. Just when I thought I had him coming my way, he would shake his head and take off again, peeling out my line at will.

When I finally brought him close to the boat, we realized this was no jack crevalle. He was wider across the back and lacked the blunt face of the crevalle. Shelly made a perfect gaff and heaved the lunker into the boat. It was a beautiful silver-bodied fish with dark yellow streaks across the top of the eyes. Yellow showed also on the forked tail. The fish's length was a good three and one-half feet, and it weighed about 40 pounds. It had the shape of a fleshy, relatively bone free fish, indicating good table fare. I thought I knew what it was, but was afraid to commit myself. We plowed back into the feeding frenzy several more times and ended up boating five of the mysterious large fish.

Back at Trade Winds Pier, we proudly showed off our fish, which when held out by the tail reached to the deck of the pier. The catch did create some excitement and commotion, but no one was willing to identify the fish. Cleaning our catch proved our guess to be true. Large boneless filets of white meat were cut from the backbones, and divided into smaller pieces.

At home in Thomasville, Georgia, I described the fish to other fishermen. The prevailing opinion, which coincided with mine, was *amberjack*, although few if any that size had ever been brought into Ochlocknee Bay. One so-called specialist in marine matters ventured that the fish were Pacific yellowtails, which had mysteriously migrated into the Gulf of Mexico.

I heard no more about amberjacks or yellowtails for three or four years until the Air Force built a circle of towers in the Gulf in 60 to 80 feet of water. Big amberjack began taking up residence at the towers, which attracted many kinds of baitfish. It then became more common to see the lunkers brought in to shore, and fancy seafood restaurants began serving grilled amberjack as a popular specialty.

That first encounter with flocks of flying fish and great wakes was a new experience for me, showing that in fishing as well as in life, *there is always something exciting and satisfying waiting there ahead of us.*

Back at Trade Winds Pier, we proudly showed off our fish.

CHAPTER 4

God's Word Changes Lives

For the word of God is living and active, sharper than any two edged sword, piercing to the division of soul and spirit...
Hebrews 4:12a RSV
In the beginning was the Word, and the Word was with God, and the Word was God. He was in the beginning with God. John 1:1,2 RSV
And the life I now live in the flesh I live by faith in the Son of God...Galatians 2:20b RSV

Somehow during my college years and for sometime thereafter I regarded Christianity as a set of moral laws, which, if observed, would produce a society of kinder and gentler people. This belief was not very different from the Pharisees, a Jewish sect, who believed that following the Law was the way to salvation. I attended church regularly, but my faith was not firm.

About this time I was asked to teach the adult class in my church. The study selected was Paul's letter to the Galatians. I wasn't sure I'd ever read Galatians, but I was sure I had no credentials for teaching it. When confronted with such a situation, there is only one thing to do. Get out the Bible, find a good commentary and cram for the exam.

The remarkable story of Paul (first called Saul) was revealed to me. He had been trained from childhood to uphold the Pharisaic laws and traditions. After graduating from the university at Tarsus, the young Pharisee pursued his ambitious plan to climb to the top of the Jewish religious hierarchy. The fastest way to achieve that goal was to apply his energy and talent toward eliminating every threat to Judaism. His drive and fiery rhetoric resulted in his appointment to wipe out the new sect later called Christians. He apparently used every means at his disposal including murder and imprisonment.

Paul had been trained by the best rabbis of his time. I could identify with that. In college I had read many of the great philosophers. I thought I had most of the answers. But a strange thing happened to Paul. On his way to Damascus to arrest followers of the Way, he was struck down by a great light, blinded and addressed by the risen Lord. He discovered that he didn't have the right answers. In fact, he was fighting on the wrong side.

What ensued was undoubtedly the greatest conversion in history. Paul was changed from the chief persecutor of the followers of Jesus to the leading evangelist and defender of the Gospel. In a vision to Ananias, a Christian disciple, Jesus said, "… he (Paul) is an instrument whom I have chosen to bring my name before Gentiles and kings and before the people of Israel. I myself will show him how much he must suffer for the sake of my name."[1]

Paul later traveled all over the Mediterranean world, establishing churches and debating Jews and Gentiles alike. He was stoned, scourged, shipwrecked, and imprisoned, but nothing could daunt his enthusiastic faith in Jesus Christ and his miraculous drive to spread the Gospel.

My study and teaching of Paul's letter began to change my life—nothing approaching the change in Paul, but a very definite change nevertheless. I realized that the moral laws, in which I had placed my trust, had never really worked in my own life. It was true that, like Paul, I knew right from wrong. I just couldn't put it into practice. Neither would any number of good deeds make up for the wrongs I had committed, soothe my guilty conscience, or keep me pointed in right direction. What a dilemma!

While majoring in political science I kept searching for a political system or philosophy which would give me a *satisfying way of life*, sort of a framework in which to live, work, and relate to others. And although I had studied many of the writers from Socrates to Karl Marx, I was perhaps just overeducated and unfulfilled. Could it be that a first century Jewish convert to the Way would furnish the answers I was seeking?

Paul's letter to the Galatians had one central theme: salvation comes through faith in Jesus Christ—not by trying to obey the Law. Paul had convinced much of the civilized world that the Gospel was the only way. Now he was convincing me.

What I had been missing was evident. I had no personal relationship with Jesus Christ. That discovery gave me an insatiable appetite for New Testament scripture. I began a journey which carried me to Christian retreats and Faith Alive weekends. Somewhere in that process my attraction to Jesus turned to trust and love. Most of us have no sudden miraculous conversion. Rather it is a gradual journey, usually however, requiring at least a gentle push, which in my case was *reading and studying the Word of God.*

Paul was struck down by a great light, blinded and addressed by the risen Lord.

Have you ever awakened in the morning feeling weighted down by "things done and things left undone?" We all either consciously or subconsciously carry a heavy burden of unremitted sins. Sooner or later these misdeeds and oversights take their toll on us squelching our joy and dragging our lives down. That's why the cross of Christ is so crucial. He took upon himself all our sins and iniquity and submitted to the punishment of suffering and dying on the cross.

Isaiah had prophesied 700 years before Christ, " But he was wounded for our transgressions, crushed for our iniquities, upon him was the punishment that made us whole, and by his bruises we are healed. All we like sheep have gone astray; we have all turned to our own way, and the Lord has laid on him the iniquity of us all."[2]

Following the perfect will of God, Jesus paid the price for our sins—to give us a fresh start. As the resurrected Son of God, He wants to lead us to a new and fuller life of service both now and in eternity. This Way satisfied me and made it easy to accept Him as Master and Savior, to try to please Him in every part of my life. What a difference from trying to follow the Law!

My conversion was indeed the *beginning* of a new, more abundant life. I would falter and fall short, but I would always feel His presence and grace, His readiness to forgive a penitent heart. It opened the possibility of breaking free from the bonds, snares, and temptations of secular culture. It eventually provided the means of dealing with a guilty conscience. It would give me the right answers, the only ones that really count in our brief sojourn through this life.

[1]Acts 9:15b,16 NRSV (author's parenthesis)
[2] Isaiah 53:5,6 NRSV

'But he was wounded for our transgressions, crushed for our iniquities, upon him was the punishment that made us whole...' Isaiah 53:5

CHAPTER 5

One of the Right Answers

Bring the full tithe into the storehouse, so that there may be food in my house, and thus put me to the test, says the Lord of hosts; see if I will not open the windows of heaven for you and pour down for you an overflowing blessing. Malachi 3:10 NRSV
There is great gain in godliness and contentment; for we brought nothing into the world and we cannot take anything out of the world. 1 Timothy 6:6,7 RSV

Either as a reward or punishment for teaching the adult class, I was chosen to head the Every Member Canvas. This was our church's method of collecting the resources needed for its annual program and budget. Being young and full of energy I felt up to any job.

The only experience I had for this task was a minor role in the previous year's canvas. I had been given five cards to work and had dutifully called upon the families, holding out my hat. Some received me cordially, while others took the occasion to beat up on me with trivial gripes about the church. Some threw every lame excuse in the book at me. It was not an edifying experience, to say the least.

For these reasons, I felt there must be a better way—one which reflected a true Christian approach. About that time I picked up a copy of Reader's Digest, which featured an article called something like, "The Modern Day Tithe." What a discovery! The idea was simple enough. Starting with the Biblical principle of tithing, the article explained that today the government carries out many of the functions exercised by the ancient Jews. The formula consisted of setting aside a tenth of one's income after taxes. That tenth could then be used to give to the church and worthwhile charities.

The idea was controversial. A few thought the church should get more, but many others wouldn't even entertain the idea of giving up ten percent of their income. However, I went ahead and we conducted the campaign on that principle. And while it wasn't the whole answer, it nevertheless established the tithe as a goal for all to work toward or at least think about. My efforts got the attention of our bishop, and before I could say no, I found myself head of the Stewardship Commission of the Episcopal Diocese of Georgia.

But I was just beginning to learn about Christian stewardship. My education continued when the bishop sent me to Baltimore, Maryland, for Christian stewardship training. We thoroughly studied the Biblical references to tithing, and the standard of ten percent was forcefully impressed on my mind. In many cases it represented the minimum. However that ten- percent, either before or after taxes, had to go to the church. Giving to charities would have to come next as a freewill offering.

We were taught that families who couldn't initially do that much should set up the tithe as a goal and reach it as quickly as possible. I have found that accepting the tithe as a minimum works and leaves me feeling good about my resource management. Tithing also has a strange way of making our resources go further and our budget process easier.

A surprise came when our instructor passed out slips of paper as the conference closed. He asked us to write down that portion of our resources that should be committed to God. He wrote down the answer and waited for us to finish. Many different percentages came in. Then he passed around the answer. To everyone's astonishment, he had written down 100 percent. He then explained to us that God is interested in every dollar we spend. We should spend it all in a Godly way, being careful not to exercise irresponsible or conspicuous consumption, excessive self-gratification, or spending that could actually hurt others or support the enemies of God.

In his book, *The Eternity Portfolio*, Alan Gotthardt expresses another valid idea about our giving for purposes of mercy and Christian evangelism. All such giving goes to building our portfolio in eternity, in heaven. We can't take our wealth with us, but it's a great feeling to build that portfolio, which will never suffer from recession, falling interest rates, or a fluctuating stock market.

The greater surprise was that my meager efforts taught me one of the great principles of Christian living—how to manage all my resources and responsibilities effectively. I was just getting started in our family's small lumber business after spending several fruitless years trying to raise cattle. The pressure was on me to make a success in my second business venture. I worked hard and fortunately had some very good associates. In a few years we revitalized and expanded the business and began to reap the rewards. We were experiencing the benefits of the free enterprise system and the entrepreneurial spirit.

But difficult questions had to be answered. How much of our profit should be shared with our employees? How far could we go in granting health insurance and retirement benefits? How was I to deal with hardship cases among our employees? Were we creating any environmental problems, and if so, how could they be abated? How could we set aside a part of our earnings to benefit community and other charities? There is no perfect answer to these questions, but I needed a framework to guide my decisions.

Again, I discovered the answer in the principle of Christian stewardship, which maintains that we never really possess anything. Material assets are merely entrusted to us by the One who created it all. We are held totally responsible to Him for the way in which we manage these resources. It's amazing how this concept clears the air and points the way toward settling difficult issues.

Risk taking is part of any business enterprise, but the most important risk I found was trusting the Owner, in this case the Creator. In business as well as in life, we sometimes have to trust

His leading even if we can't clearly see the outcome. Taking this risk is an essential part of stewardship. Once determining the Lord's leading, I have never been disappointed in the end result.

After my father passed away, the leadership of our land company passed on to me. Timberlands especially fit into the stewardship concept. It has helped guide me to good ecological practices— planting trees and properly harvesting timber in order to pay regular cash distributions to the partners. This practice was carried on without ever depleting the timber as we were always growing more than we cut. I, of course, had great help from my associates and from what my father had taught me. It was always his creed to leave the land in better condition than when he acquired it. He passed that principle on to me, and it was validated in my understanding of Christian stewardship.

The concept of Christian stewardship greatly assisted me on my journey and made my pathway toward the abundant life much easier.

CHAPTER 6

A Different Way to Catch Big Fish

One of the exciting things about life is making new discoveries. In fact, the activities we engage in would get pretty dull without them. I was introduced to a *new concept in the art of fishing one summer at Amelia Island, Florida. It bore little resemblance to the ordered way of fishing from a boat.*

I had a friend, George Rumpel, who lived at Ponte Vedra Beach, Florida. He had done some cost accounting for our company, and when I learned that he was an enthusiastic fisherman, our friendship became closer. One day he related to me what sounded like a preposterous tale about red fishing in the surf at Amelia Island. Since my family was planning to spend our vacation there the following summer, he invited me to fish with him.

Our close friends, the James Day family, shared a cottage with us that summer. James was one of my fishing pals who was always eager for a fishing adventure.

James and I met George before day under the bridge that crosses Nassau Sound just south of Amelia Island. There was a broken down fish house close to the water, run by a middle-aged woman and her young daughter. George possessed only a small outboard motor, so we rented a leaky old skiff and headed for the islands in the Sound. A pretty good breeze was blowing that morning and the moderate chop made me a little nervous, especially since we were headed for the open sea.

George's plan, however, was to run to the back of each island away from the sea, anchor the boat, and taking our rigs and bait, hike across the island to fish in the open surf. The tide was rising when we came to *Bird Island*, the largest in the Sound. We executed this maneuver with no trouble and were soon fishing in the waves breaking against the island. Our bait was an ample strip of fresh mullet, which we cast out as far as we could, using the bottom lead to carry it. We were all standing in water about knee deep, fighting off occasional big waves.

The action came much quicker than I expected. I was using a loose line (with the drag off) when something picked up my bait and ran about thirty feet before I could close the drag and set the hook. When I did, the big fish hardly slowed at all. Instead, he pealed off forty yards of my line with my reel screaming. What a tantalizing moment that was. The fish was headed for open water, and I was trying to slow him down with a small Ambassador reel. He then turned to circle, which saved my remaining line. As he did, I slowly began to gain a few feet on him. I was beginning to feel more comfortable when he made another run, taking my line back again.

This scene repeated itself three times before the big fish began to tire and come my way. When I finally brought him close enough to glimpse, I was stunned. The redfish was almost three feet long, weighing between fifteen and twenty pounds. I led him to the beach and pulled him up on the sand. I then strung the live red on my fish string, tied it around my waist and returned to the fishing. Every once in a while the big red would brush against my leg giving me an eerie feeling.

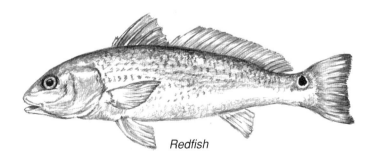

Redfish

That was the first of nine bull reds we caught that day. Each island we fished was smaller than Bird, and the last one was knee deep in water, which made anchoring the boat and stepping out a little tricky. We caught one or more reds off each island. This fishing discovery led to many more exciting trips in the years that followed, and established George as the consummate redfish guide.

In fishing, life, and faith it pays to keep in mind that we never really know it all. Paul expressed it this way, "For now we see in a mirror dimly, but then face to face. Now I know in part; then I shall understand fully…" [1]

[1]1st Corinthians 13:12a RSV

We ran the boat to the back of each island and hiked across to fish in the open surf.

CHAPTER 7

The Holy Spirit Sparks
the Flame of Renewal

In the last days it will be, God declares, that I will pour out my Spirit upon all flesh, and your sons and your daughters shall prophesy...
Acts 2:17a NRSV
My speech and my proclamation were not with plausible words of wisdom, but with a demonstration of the Spirit and of power, so that your faith might rest not on human wisdom but on the power of God.
1st Corinthians 2:4,5 NRSV

I thought I was doing pretty well on my Christian journey. I was singing in the choir, teaching Sunday school, serving on the governing board of our church, and even serving the bishop on various commissions. I had made my commitment to the Lord. Then one day I was confronted by a lady in our congregation. She was not at all "moony," off the wall, or even fundamentalist. In fact, she was a recognized and respected community leader as well as a leader in our church.

She put it to me this way: *"Would you believe that there is more, much more than you have already experienced?"* I didn't really know what she was talking about, and she didn't try to explain it right then. But she did provide opportunities for me to discover it in the weeks to come.

The Episcopal Church is liturgical. That means that there is a stated order to worship services. These services are written in the Book of Common Prayer, which is based upon the Bible and the experience of the church through the ages following the Apostolic Period. In fact the service itself is called a liturgy. The principal service is Holy Communion during which every member of the congregation comes forward and partakes from a common cup of wine and receives a small wafer in remembrance of the Last Supper. It is a beautiful service, which brings to mind (or to the present) the sacrifice that Jesus made for us.

What more could any Christian want? Each Communion can be a very moving experience. That's exactly where I was until I began attending a small prayer and praise service in a comfortably furnished room in our church. First of all, there was no stated order to this service. We opened by singing contemporary praise music, accompanied by a guitar. The melodies were pleasant and the words all came from Bible passages.

After twenty minutes of this kind of praise, the music stopped and there was a period of silence until someone was moved to pray—not a written prayer but one straight from the heart. This was followed by other prayers or short Scripture offerings. These were sometimes interspersed with a Christian song sung a cappella and started spontaneously by a member of the group. Although there was no structure to the service, it always flowed along as if directed by an unseen Spirit.

If a member of the group needed prayer or desired prayer for someone not present, all members would gather around and lay their hands on the person's head or shoulders. Prayers would be made spontaneously always in the name of Jesus Christ.

There was a period open for prophecy. If any member felt a strong urging, a message of encouragement, comfort, or sometimes exhortation would be given, preceded by the statement, "I believe God is telling us..." The meeting would close with a joyful and spirited Christian song.

Although I am a life long Episcopalian, I found the service especially moving and satisfying. I even felt a strange lifting of my spirit, a glow something like the effects of alcohol, except ever so much better. (I recall people thinking that the disciples at Pentecost must have been filled with new wine.)

This was my introduction to the Renewal Movement of the 60s

and 70s. It would never, of course, replace the liturgy of the Episcopal Church, but it would complement it greatly. My renewal worship experience also gave me a heightened joy and appreciation for liturgical worship. But none of this can be adequately described; it must be experienced.

The Renewal Movement starting in the 60s became one of the great revivals of God's church. No one outstanding leader started it, and no one leader became its chief advocate. The most unusual thing about it was its spontaneous start in many different denominations including the Roman Catholic Church. This unintentional activity led many people to believe that the advocate was indeed the Holy Spirit of God.

Many Christians believe that salvation comes by being born again in the Spirit. Jesus said, " Truly, truly, I say to you, unless one is born again, he cannot see the kingdom of God."[1] In answer to Nicodemus's question Jesus states that one must be born of water and the Spirit in order to enter the Kingdom. These remarks were early in his ministry, long before he talked about the Spirit to his disciples.

Problems arise when the gifts of the Spirit are discussed or manifested. According to Paul these include healing, discernment, prophecy, speaking in tongues, teaching, administration, and others. The Renewal Movement was accompanied by many of these gifts. Comfortable church members were shaken up by the gifts.

I never had that problem, relying on Paul's statement in 1st Corinthians, chapter 12. "To each is given the manifestation of the Spirit for the common good. To one is given through the Spirit the utterance of wisdom, and to another the utterance of knowledge according to the same Spirit, to another faith by the same Spirit, to another gifts of healing by the one Spirit, to another the working of miracles, to another prophesy, to another the discernment of spirits, to another various kinds of tongues, to another the interpretation of tongues. All these are activated by one and the same Spirit, *who allots to each one individually just as the Spirit chooses.*"[2]

33

The first great split in the Christian church was between the Eastern Orthodox Branch centered in Constantinople and the Western Church headquartered in Rome. The tradition of the Western Church was eventually heavily influenced by scientific rationalism, which tended to de-emphasize the supernatural.[3] The Eastern Church was not as subject to this influence. Consequently the church in the West including the Protestant denominations tended to lose faith in contemporary, supernatural acts of God. This tradition has carried over largely into the churches in America.

I believe this is a principal reason that supernatural acts of the Holy Spirit are sometimes misunderstood. But God's Holy Spirit is not to be denied. He will bring about the supernatural because it is within His power and authority to do so. And He will always shake up His church with these acts—especially when He perceives that we need to witness them in order to experience His great power and grace.

It is possible to use the gifts inappropriately, so one test is whether or not they edify the Body of Christ, the Christian church. For instance, tongues even with interpretation can be most confusing to a visitor. This led Paul to say, "I thank God that I speak in tongues more than you all, nevertheless in church I would rather speak five words with my mind, in order to instruct others, than ten thousand words in a tongue." [4]

I believe prophecies can be more effectively given in common language for the edification of the Body. Paul further states, "For those who speak in a tongue do not speak to other people but to God, for nobody understands them, since they are speaking mysteries in the Spirit. On the other hand, those who prophesy speak to other people for their upbuilding and encouragement, and consolation. Those who speak in a tongue build up themselves, but those who prophesy build up the church." [5]

I would like to relate my experience with speaking in tongues. I do this with great humility and even greater fear that I might be misunderstood. There was a time in my life when I was asked to take on a serious responsibility. I was unsure as to whether I had the strength of faith and ability to carry it out. It was under these conditions that I prayed late into the night for God to give me a special filling of the Holy Spirit with the gift of tongues. In my weakness I felt I needed that gift for reassurance in accepting the challenge.

He blessed me by answering my prayer. Since then I have used the gift, sparingly, in private prayer and on occasions when praying

"...I will pour out my Spirit upon all flesh..." Acts 2:17a

for a sick person when I didn't know what to pray for. Essentially for me, "tongues" is a prayer language, which I occasionally use when speaking to God. It has served principally to build me up when I needed it most, and I hope it has served indirectly to build up the church. I know that my view is not Pentecostal in the strict sense, but I believe with Paul that the gift is one of many which the Holy Spirit *allots to each one individually just as the Spirit chooses.*[6]

I have certainly witnessed many instances of other gifts, which in a sense are much more important since they tend to build up the church in a direct manner. I have heard anointed preaching and teaching which were more than just good. The anointing of the Spirit was definitely there. Anointed service music has moved me to tears. I have experienced the anointing upon people who always open their homes for church functions and have a special quality of hospitality. I have known people who put their service to the Lord before all other calls upon their lives. I have felt comforted and built up by words of prophecy. And I have observed anointed qualities of leadership and administration in God's church.

Addressing the gift of healing, I have found prayers for healing to be more efficacious when using the method outlined by James: calling the elders of the church together to pray over the sick, anointing them with oil in the name of the Lord. This is not possible in every situation, so other types of healing prayer can be effective. I am part of a prayer chain in our church, who communicate by phone the moment prayers are needed. This method assures that many people are praying the same healing prayers when they are needed the most. Also I believe that prayers at the altar or side altar during Holy Communion can be effective.

When God's church becomes too comfortable, self-serving, and complacent, I believe He wakes us up with the great power of the Holy Spirit. Revival results—sometimes worldwide. Apostolic practices are *rediscovered.* This is how I view the Renewal Movement of the last few decades of the 20th Century. I am most fortunate to have encountered it on my journey. *My life was changed and blessed* by prayer and praise services, by small group accountability meetings, by daily encounters with God in prayer and scripture and by regular intercession for others. The Holy Spirit is alive and active in the church—thanks be to God.

[1]John 3:3b NASB
[2]1st Corinthians 12:7-11 NRSV
[3]Hummel, Charles E., *Fire in the Fireplace, Charismatic Renewal in the 90's.* Downer's Grove, Ill. 1993 p. 125
[4]1st Corinthians 14:18,19 RSV
[5]1st Corinthians 14:2-4 NRSV
[6]1st Corinthians 12:11b NRSV

CHAPTER 8

Baby Helps Me Refocus
My Fishing Practices

Approaching seventy-six years of age, I found that I could no longer pull off the physical requirements needed for most fishing expeditions. I can manage, with the help of my pals, to trailer my 16-foot bass boat from Thomasville to the Aucilla River. From there we fish close to shore, around the points, saltwater creeks, and the river itself in the cool months, and no more than three miles offshore during the summer.

But from our cottage at St. George Island, Fla., the situation is quite different. As strange as it sounds, there are no good public ramps on the island, and so launching a boat becomes a real problem. There is a marvelous State Park on the east end of St. George, presenting the public with beautiful white sand beaches and a couple of fair boat ramps. Even these launching places pose a difficult problem at low tides.

So what is a septuagenarian like me supposed to do? Surfcasting is a possibility, but this sport at the island yields very little return. And I had given up fishing offshore in a big boat years before. *A refocusing of my island fishing practices was called for.*

I found the answer three years ago. I happened to be passing through a small town on Highway 84 west of Thomasville when I spotted a 13- foot riveted aluminum boat with an electric motor on the bow. I turned around, and after talking price with the owner, I became the proud father of the small craft, which I named *Baby*. Some weeks later I purchased a 9.9 horse Johnson motor for the stern, and I was ready to go back to the basics of saltwater fishing.

Now, don't misunderstand me. *Baby* was not built for most saltwater fishing and certainly not for any chop higher than 18 inches, but I had a special kind of situation in mind. If launched from one of the Park ramps on St. George, I could maneuver in the Goose Island Bay, and on calm days even venture out on the big Apalachicola Bay. When I did dare to test the big bay, I would stay close to the Island, so I could beach the tiny craft if necessary. But the best feature of Baby is her weight. Two weak old men can almost pick her up, making the launching a piece of cake. *By God's grace I had discovered a way to keep on fishing from the island.*

There are many oyster bars in Apalachicola Bay and from Goose Island to the East End there are many areas of grass flats that attract speckled trout, blue fish, and some big reds. Quite by luck I found one area no larger than a tennis court that usually held a good population of the three above species and even included flounder, Spanish mackerel, and an occasional tarpon. Of course, I can't divulge the specific location. To do so would break the Fisherman's Code, which states that the best way to deplete honey from a honey hole is to divulge its location.

I have enjoyed many of these simple and basic fishing trips, this past summer being no exception. My best trip included my pal, Dan Hardman, who is certainly no old man, having fought as a Marine in Vietnam. And even though I usually fish with people my own age, youthful strength and elder experience make a pretty nice combination.

On that particular occasion, we were on time well before day at the boat ramp. Darkness makes it easier for me to catch live pinfish and fingerling mullet with my throw net. After catching an ample supply of live bait, we launched *Baby*, and headed for the honey hole. Normally the bright orange ball of sun is just beginning to peek over the horizon as we arrive. But on this day a large cloud obscured the sun for an hour or two. That did nothing to hurt the fishing.

On our first drift, Dan hooked up with a big red and fought it almost to the boat before it pulled off the hook. That's always disappointing, but he got a reprieve on the very next drift and brought a 26-inch red to the boat. After landing it, we continued

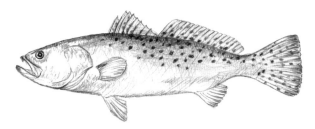

Speckled Trout or Spotted Sea Trout

our drift and my red Greedy Gut cork went under. I set my hook in a 22 inch speckled trout and had him alongside the boat in less than three minutes. We caught three more large trout and one blue on the next two drifts. Catching a blue, a red and a trout qualified Dan for a Florida "inshore slam" T-shirt, which was later conferred on him at the bait store.

When we drifted back over the area where the large reds had struck, Dan was generous and let me hook the next red, which took straight off with most of my line. I shouted instructions to Dan to start the motor and follow the fish, but I had failed to familiarize him with the engine. While he was fumbling around under my anxious directions, the big fish turned and gave me back some line. I then relieved my pal from motor duty while I fought the lunker toward the boat.

The really strange thing about this trip was that the school of reds never moved very far from the same spot. Dan hooked another large one and boated it, requiring the Captain to administer artificial respiration before releasing it. No, I didn't breath into its mouth. I simply held it in front of the large tail and worked it back and forth, forcing water through the gills. As I felt it come to life, I gradually released my grip and the great fish swam off, perhaps to thrill another angler on another day.

I believe we could have caught any number of the bull reds, but since one fish per person is the limit, we moved away from the school. The last fish we caught was a large flounder, weighing close to four pounds. That put the icing on the cake, and two tired but happy fishermen headed for shore. *Baby* had made me a proud father again, *confirming my new method of island fishing.*

40

Catching live pinfish and fingerling mullet with my throw net.

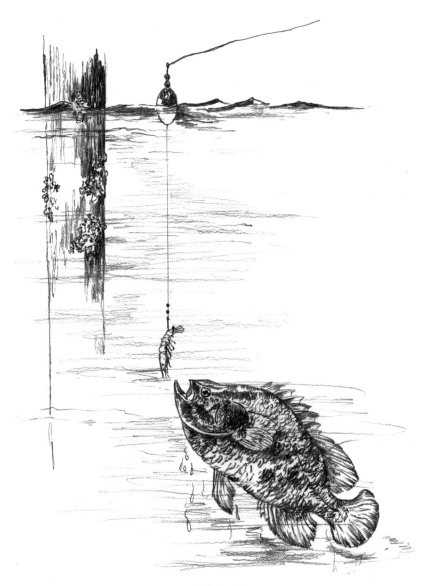

Tripletail

CHAPTER 9

Seeking the Mysterious Tripletail

The tripletail is a mystery fish to most saltwater anglers. It doesn't really have three tails. Large slanted top and bottom fins coupled with a large tail make it look that way. I had heard numerous tales about these saltwater residents, but I had never even seen one, much less caught one. They were pictured to me as a kind of saltwater sunfish, generally shaped like a freshwater bream, but much larger. The description put the weight at 10 to 20 pounds, but I felt this had to be a fanciful fish tale.

I first discovered tripletails about 30 miles offshore. I was fishing with my favorite deep-sea fishing guide, Larry Tucker. We had gone offshore from Ochlocknee Bay looking for large floating islands of Sargasso grass reportedly in the area. We found the grass but the schooling dolphin fish were nowhere to be seen.

It was then that Larry spotted a flock of man-o-war birds circling in formation. This bird in itself is a curiosity. Usually seen far offshore, they are large dark birds with tremendous wingspans. The wingspan alone makes them easy to identify, but a closer look reveals rakish looking, angled wings. The clincher is the scissors shaped tail. Called the Magnificent Frigatebird, it can soar on wind currents with little effort, which is what the flock was doing a quarter-mile from our boat.

On the ocean, circling or diving birds usually spell fish. We quickly motored over and sure enough, schooling dolphin fish of all sizes began darting under our boat. In the water dolphin fish (not porpoises) have a bright, phosphorescent blue color. Once pulled on board the color quickly fades to dull green with yellow markings. We had a great time catching dolphin. The only problem was that when we hooked a big one, it would strip off line and dive into the thick Sargasso, making it impossible to catch.

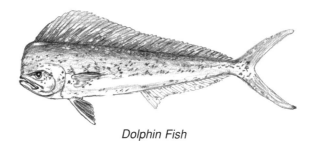

Dolphin Fish

When we left the Sargasso and started in, we checked several isolated plots of grass for fish. At a mixture of flotsam and grass we discovered a school of small black colored pan fish. Larry guessed they were tripletails and he turned out to be right. When we floated small pieces of bait to them, they would strike without fear. I took a good look at the first one pulled on board and it fit the description of the tripletail perfectly except for size. Its shape was almost identical to a very large blue gill bream.

It was several years later before I even heard the name tripletail mentioned again. It seems that during the warm months the larger fish come close to shore and take up residence around buoys and piling. Apalachicola Bay, Florida, then becomes a favorite fishing ground for tripletail anglers. But there aren't many such people since, as one of my old fishing pals used to say, " it's more of an *intellectual* pursuit." That's "fishese" meaning, "they're scarce and very hard to come by."

My favorite Apalach guide, Rex Phipps, had just given our party a good morning with the trout and reds, when I asked him about tripletails. He gave me sort of a sideways smile, and asked if I really wanted to try it. When I insisted, he began instructing us in the basics. First, only one person can fish at a time. Then he instructed us to keep the cork real close or butting the piling at all times. He would manage the boat and keep it in position. (His facetious remarks had me thinking of a midnight snipe hunt at Boy Scout camp.) We decided to take turns at each buoy or piling.

After trying a dozen markers, we came up empty, and the word, *intellectual* came sharply back in focus. However, when my turn came around again, I grabbed the rod, put on a small live menhaden and cast it out. It hit the piling and fell into the water. I carefully maneuvered the cork so that it kept butting against the piling.

I had no great expectation when I noticed the cork had gone under. I gave it a second or two and set the hook. It was like I had hooked into a small log, except this log was alive and swimming away. Rex quickly maneuvered the boat away from the piling, and I had a real fight on my hands. When the fish turned side ways, I could not move him at all and just had to let him "sull." Then I would gain a foot or two of line as he turned back. He made no big runs but pulled like a large bulldog.

I finally fought him close to the boat and Rex netted him. He was indeed a large tripletail going more than ten pounds. We all admired the fish and Rex made it even better by describing the table quality of the catch.

That was my first big tripletail. I discovered that fishing for them requires experience, much patience and some precise maneuvering, *but hey!* Doesn't life require the same?

Part Three

TRIALS…

A life without trials and tests has little chance of building character and faith. None of us invite these times, but God has a way of testing us for our own great good. Fishing has its share of trials as well, and while we don't enjoy the moment, we often look back with more than a few hearty chuckles.

CHAPTER 10

A Clouded Fishing Trip

We were approaching the end of Dog Days, that season of late summer when it's not a question of whether it will rain, but rather what time of day it will come and how much. We had been in a wet year for a change, with a surplus of several inches of rain. This had a profound effect on our fishing. The coastal waters around the Aucilla and Econfina Rivers in Florida were dark with tannic acid flowing from hardwood forests. As the days went on, this condition prevailed as far as five miles offshore. Even the redfish, which have a high tolerance for fresh water, had moved out of the area, making our catches improbable. It was under these extreme conditions that Cutter and I decided we needed to visit the coast, fish or no fish.

Cutter Knapp, besides being one of my life-long friends is also my regular fishing pal. Cutter has many ocean going qualifications, one of which is his service in the U.S. Navy on a destroyer, commonly called a Tin Can. He's a guy who quickly makes friends with everyone he meets and even remembers their names, a good qualification for his service as a county commissioner. He also wields a pretty good rod and reel.

We had a late tide, so we left Thomasville at 7:45 AM, an hour later than usual. A funny thing happened to us on the way to the coast. As we turned onto the four-lane just out of town, we saw a very high white cloud to our south in an otherwise blue and cloudless sky. At first we paid little attention to it, but the further we traveled, the same cloud stayed far to our south. We then began to speculate about its position. It's sixty-five miles from my house to the Aucilla River landing, probably more like 45 as the crow flies. That's a long way to see a cloud, but half way down, the same cloud kept looming directly to our south.

At each curve in the road we kept hoping that the cloud was located to our east or west. But when we arrived at JR's Aucilla River Store, the cloud loomed menacingly behind it. Its base had now broadened and begun to darken. After stocking up on drinks and bait, we drove to the landing to launch the boat. I happened to walk to the river's edge, and there the cloud was, right in the mouth of the Aucilla River. Its base was now black and seemed to be moving toward us.

There was nothing to do but kill some time and let the rainstorm do its thing, so we left the landing and drove to Nuttall Rise to see our friend, Jack Simpson. I had a message to deliver to him from an old friend, so we could kill two birds with one stone. Jack invited us in and we had a good visit before he went to his computer to get the radar screen. Fortunately the radar showed the storm moving west, so we returned to the River and launched my boat, the *Black Hole*. (The name derives from the vast sum of money I manage to spend on a small 16-foot bass boat.)

I ran wide open to the River mouth and halfway out to our baitfish traps, about two miles offshore. We found plenty of live pinfish in our traps and set out to the GPS location where we had caught fish the week before. An hour of drifting with live pinfish under our Cajun Thunder corks yielded us nothing but a half-dozen sail cats. The cloud had moved far to our west and a light breeze sprang up, giving us a good drift. I then made the decision to move farther offshore.

The water in our new position was a little clearer, but still showed some dark stain. I scored first with a small 17-inch trout. We boated and released more sail cats and a few sharks, but it seemed the good fish had moved away or developed lockjaw. Then it happened. Cutter got a good strike, with the fish peeling off most of his line on the first run. I pulled in my rigs and lowered the motor to follow the fish. We soon caught up with him, giving Cutter the slack he needed to retrieve some line. The fish immediately took off again, turning the boat in his direction, and we followed. We speculated about what the lunker might be, and Cutter swore that he had to be five or six feet long.

This happened three times before we finally drew close to him again. This time Cutter remarked, "I believe he's tiring out." And sure enough he came to the top, and as he came into view, I literally gasped at the size! A mere 15 inches long, it wasn't even a decent undersized gag grouper. When such things happen, speculation really runs rife. Maybe there were two fish on the same hook, the large one pulling off at the last minute. Maybe the mama grouper was holding onto her baby's tail. Or maybe that baby fish got hold of some atomic waste that made it a super-duper grouper.

Well, that sarcastic speculation died when Cutter got another strike and began a hard ten-minute fight. This time the right colors showed as the cobia turned sideways flashing his white streak. He measured exactly 33 inches to the fork in the tail and weighed a good twenty pounds.

The cloud that had threatened us all morning, even as we left home, had been lifted, giving us a good day on the Gulf with all the exciting surprises of saltwater fishing.

We saw a very high white cloud to our south in an otherwise blue and cloudless sky.

CHAPTER 11

Lifting the Cloud of Illness

Say to those who are of a fearful heart, "Be strong, fear not! Behold, your God will come with vengeance, with the recompense of God. He will come and save you." Then the eyes of the blind shall be opened, and the ears of the deaf unstopped; then shall the lame man leap like a hart and the tongue of the dumb sing for joy. For waters shall break forth in the wilderness, and streams in the desert; the burning sand shall become a pool, and the thirsty ground springs of water. Isaiah 35:4-7a RSV

We live much of our lives as if in a bubble. Inside the bubble are our egos, our preferences, our goals, our families, our friends, our careers, and our pleasures. Outside the bubble is the Holy Spirit of God—all around us but not penetrating. As long as things are going our way and we are content with enjoying life, the bubble is not penetrated and we are content with the status quo.

But somewhere on our journey things turn sour. We come up against a situation we cannot cope with. We find that in reality we are weak and that none of our life experiences has prepared us for this moment. We seek the consolation and assistance of friends and, if ill, medical science. It is then that we confront the startling fact that our bubble must be penetrated. We are no longer sufficient in our own strength to contend with life.

Paul in 2nd Corinthians tells us what we need to understand, what the Lord told him, "My grace is sufficient for you, *for power is made perfect in weakness."* (Paul then confesses) 'So, I will boast all the more gladly of my weaknesses, so that the power of Christ may dwell in me. Therefore I am content with weaknesses, insults, hardships, persecutions, and calamities for the sake of Christ; *for whenever I am weak, then I am strong.'* [1]

It is often in the time of desperate weakness that we finally attempt to punch a hole in the bubble. God is punching through from the other side. We are reaching for Him and He is reaching for us. Michelangelo painted it on the ceiling of the Sistine Chapel. The contact is what will save us. The bubble bursts as we finally realize where our strength, power, and salvation really come from. The strong presence of the Holy Spirit floods upon us, sweeping us toward the current of faith.

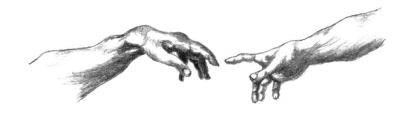

We are reaching for Him and He is reaching for us, just as Michelangelo painted it on the Sistine Chapel.

About fifteen years ago I was faced with a serious medical problem, one which my father had faced during his lifetime. It was a condition called diverticulitis or the infection of small pockets in the intestinal tract. One day at work I was doubled up with severe pain in my lower left abdomen. I was hospitalized and at 2 AM the next morning I had a colon rupture. After I had been sedated, my surgeon told me I would have to face two major operations, one to repair the damage, clean the infection, and install a colostomy. The next one would remove the colostomy and connect me up again. I had been in such pain that I welcomed any way out. The emergency operation was performed before day that same morning.

I recovered quickly from the first operation and several months later I had the second. After about ten days of intravenous antibiotics I was released from the hospital, but something inside never felt quite right. My general health again recovered quickly, but the "catch" in my left side remained. I underwent several tests and even went to a noted clinic, but nothing seemed to improve it. The condition persisted for several more months.

Seemingly faced with an incurable physical problem, from which I could get no release, I gradually slipped into depression. This condition is both mental and physical and there is no easy cure. I was literally plunged into a deep cloud of despair. I lost my appetite and could not sleep. Concentration was impossible and I could not work. At times my heart raced furiously and skipped beats. I remember not caring whether I woke up the next morning, and suicide is more than a rare ending for this condition.

I consulted counselors and a psychiatrist. I tried many prescription drugs including Prozac. I read the Psalms over and over and, for some strange reason, the only books I could read were about hopeless castaways. I really believed I would never recover. The words of the English poet, William Henley kept coming back to me, "Dark as the night that covers me, Black as the pit from pole to pole."

In my desperation, I now turned completely to the Lord for help. Our church prays for people at the side-altar every Sunday morning at the main service, so I became a regular there, asking for healing prayer. I probably visited the altar for almost a year. During this time I knew that my minister, his wife and others were praying for me each day. I held my own and perhaps grew a little better. My regular doctor, who is a very active Christian layman, made my healing complete. He prescribed an old-line antidepressant, which was rarely used anymore.

One morning I woke up and felt much better—even like going to work again and joining the human race. *The cloud had been lifted.* Even my old nemesis the "catch" was gone. I ascribe my healing first of all to the Lord and to the faithful people who prayed and never lost hope. Also I credit my Christian doctor for being given the wisdom to prescribe the right drug for me.

Now many people would not see the miraculous in my healing, mainly because it was not instantaneous. And I want to be careful to say that I believe God gives us medicine for our good health and wellness. But I do believe that medicine alone cannot always bring about a cure, and I firmly believe that God heals in many ways—one of which involves prayer and intercession. We are given directions in the book of James. "Are any among you sick? They should call for the elders of the church and have them pray over them, anointing them with oil in the name of the Lord. The prayer of faith will save the sick and the Lord will raise them up…The prayer of the righteous is powerful and effective." [2]

Since that time, I have seen many miracles of healing. A terminal cancer patient was healed by following James's prayer directions and with the medical aid of a noted cancer clinic. A patient's serious aggressive cancer was held in check for several weeks until the operation could be performed. A baby with a hole in its heart was healed. A woman with a large tumor witnessed its disappearance.

Later in life I received a report from my doctor that I had leukemia and lymphoma. It's hard to describe the feeling one gets when receiving such news. It involves denial and fear. It certainly places one's mortality on center stage. One specialist gave a dismal prognosis of only a few months. But again the spiritual life became most important, and I turned to the Lord for strength and guidance. I asked the elders of the Church to pray for me.

The right steps in my treatment were made clear to me in ways I never would have expected. The right clinic was shown to me. Even the right doctor, one of the best in his field. After I spent months trying to get an appointment, my home phone rang one afternoon. Imagine my surprise when this busy doctor asked me when I could come to the clinic. After his diagnosis involving a number of tests, he prescribed a relatively new type of chemotherapy. I took the first treatment at the clinic to determine how I would react. I was able to take the others at the oncology center in my hometown.

Weeks later I returned to the clinic and went through the same tests. The tests showed no cancer in my body. What a blessing I had received! Again I felt that my journey had been extended and I was given a chance to write and witness.

In my case, a particular scripture passage was most important:

"And a leper came to Him and bowed down before Him and said, 'Lord, if You are willing, You can make me clean.' Jesus stretched out His hand and touched him, saying, 'I am willing; be cleaned.' And immediately his leprosy was cleansed." [3]

The key expression is, "Lord, are you willing?" with the response a definitive, "I am willing." I pondered this expression day and night until I became the one asking the Lord if he was willing. I always got the same mental response, " I am willing." Nothing was more important to me during the weeks of chemotherapy.

We are all created to live for a certain life span, some longer than others, so eventually all will pass away from this life. Even those the Lord raised from the dead eventually died. But the fact remains that a very important part of the ministry of Jesus was healing the sick. According to the scripture, "When Jesus entered Peter's house he saw his (Peter's) mother-in-law lying in bed with a fever; he touched her hand, and the fever left her, and she got up and began to serve him. That evening they brought to him many who were possessed with demons; and he cast out the spirits with a word, and cured all who were sick. This was to fulfill what had been spoken through the prophet Isaiah, 'He took our infirmities and bore our diseases.' "[4]

Christians continued the practice of healing prayer on through the third or fourth century and even to the present, especially in times of revival and renewal. My journey has taught me that healing prayer is still a very important part of living the Gospel, and I commend it to all who are in need.

[1]2nd Corinthians 12:9,10 NRSV
[2]James 5:14,15a,16b NRSV
[3]Matthew 8:2,3 NASB
[4]Matthew 8:14-17 NRSV (author's parenthesis)

CHAPTER 12

It Was The Best of Fishing—
It Was The Worst of Fishing

Fishing trips are a lot like life. There are good times and bad times…

It was one of those days in late spring. Light cold fronts were still pushing into the Gulf of Mexico causing unpredictable weather. When I checked the tide, I was discouraged. Saturday morning there would be only a foot of falling tide—not exactly a prime day for fishing. When I discussed these dismal prospects with Cutter, my fishing partner, we still decided to give it a go since we were both itching to get out on the water.

Arriving at the Aucilla landing slightly after high tide, we moved out along the shoreline into a creek mouth to fish for reds. Since the shrimp at JR's store had all died the night before, the best we could present were dead and slightly spoiled bait. An hour of this activity produced three medium sized trout and an acceptable black drum. One huge red did strike only 25 feet from the boat, but we failed to get his attention. We pulled in the anchors and headed for the flats east of the Aucilla River.

There were a couple of squall lines in the Gulf, and although there was only a light breeze, I kept my eye on them. One squall moved west toward St. Marks and over the mainland. After robbing our traps we began to fish with live pinfish. Cutter was first to get a strike and pulled in a nice trout—about 20 inches. That started it off and I soon had a medium one on. That gave us five, which is one limit, before the other squall began moving our way. Sitting wrapped in our storm suits, we waited anxiously until the squall passed over us. Fortunately it had no wind, and we were soon back to fishing, with the sun peeping out.

Sometimes fish will stop biting after a squall moves over, but on this day the opposite occurred. The trout began biting again, and we soon had our second limit. I added a nice Spanish mackerel and lost a blue fish after two jumps. Then it happened. I got a good strike and the lunker took off, squealing yards of line off my reel. I yelled at Cutter to start the motor for fear of running out of line, but just as it cranked, the big fish turned and began to circle. I fought hard to regain line sometimes only a foot at a time. But I wound enough back to feel comfortable again.

Now circling about 75 feet out, I would gain some line only to lose it back. Every once in a while the monster would shake his head in redfish fashion only much harder. We both tried to guess what it was and speculation turned from a giant red to a nasty shark. When I finally pulled him within thirty feet, we strained hard to make out his color and shape. The color was not silver, which ruled out a jack crevalle or a kingfish. It was dark, almost the color of the water. We both exclaimed about the same time, "Cobia." And that's what it was, for now the fish turned on its side, showing the white line running laterally along its body.

There's no way to land a cobia that big in a fish net, but fortunately I carried along a short gaff hook, which Cutter soon found. Then I began coaching him on how to gaff the fish (which he didn't take too well). It's a serious mistake to gaff a "green" cobia. They've been known to tear up the inside of a boat. So I kept bringing the fish around only to warn, "He's still too green."

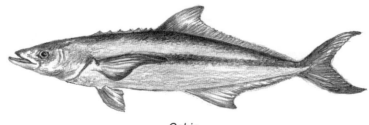

Cobia

When I did give Cutter the go ahead, he struck the fish in the mouth but missed him, and we were lucky not to pull the hook out. On the next pass he gaffed him right behind the side fins and heaved him into the boat. When I put the yardstick on him, he went 35 inches from the tip of his head to the fork of the tail—two inches over the minimum length requirement. Over all he measured a good 40 inches and probably weighed between 20 and 25 pounds.

That was the good trip, ending with the unexpected, even sensational.

The following week, Cutter and I were both eager to follow up on our luck. I related the excitement of the trip to our middleman and cookie (our gourmet lunch maker), Bill King, and had him chomping at the bit to go. Bill is my first cousin, my dentist, and normally the third member of our crew, a combination which comes in handy when a toothache strikes on the weekend. This time the tide was excellent—a good three-foot rise from early morning till midday. The weather forecast was also better. At JR's store the shrimp were fresh and trying to jump out of the tank.

We loaded for bear and headed out the Aucilla River. Before we got to the mouth, however, the wind picked up and we were soon experiencing two to three foot waves. One of my crew remarked, "Isn't this pretty rough for the river?"

I replied in my most consummate Captain's voice, "It's always rougher right in the River mouth. It'll calm down when we reach the Gulf." That remark was "rubbed in" the Captain several times as we left the River to face an unruly Gulf, full of floating grass. We should have turned back, but nothing can deter three septuagenarians, who are thinking *40 years old*—especially that close to the fishing.

We checked our fish traps and found an ample supply of pinfish. Then we made the best of it. Every time I cranked up the motor for another drift, several waves would break over the bow before I could get up on a plane. The bilge pump worked overtime and my feet were usually covered with water. Two hours of this frenetic activity and four small trout later, we decided to head to the coastline for reds, but between the endless clumps of floating grass and muddy water, the reds were too smart to be anywhere nearby. So, disappointedly, we picked up and headed back into the Aucilla.

We were well into the river when my motor almost cut off. I shifted into neutral and gunned it a couple of times before taking off again. This time the heat whistle came on and I had to stop to cool the engine. I shifted into neutral again to let water circulate, and in 20 seconds the whistle stopped. I noticed, however, that only a meager stream was squirting out of the water indicator hole, so I found my short piece of stiff wire and began jigging into the hole. This tactic usually loosens any grass that might have clogged it. On the third jig, the electric shock knocked me back onto the deck. I had been through this exercise a thousand times before, and I couldn't believe what had happened. I was so incredulous that I grabbed the wire again and... blap! I was knocked down again.

I've often heard that a small amount of electricity is good for the body so I figured I'd taken my dose for the day. The next problem was that the motor refused to crank. Well, we were sitting there helpless when a good friend from Tallahassee pulled up in his boat. He was on his way in and offered to pull us to the landing. That maneuver went well and we finally got the *Black Hole* on the trailer. My boat's reputation was really beginning to live up to its name.

We cleaned our fish and started home with Cutter deciding to take the less traveled route. We were in the middle of nowhere when Cutter remarked, "Something's wrong. We better check the trailer." I jumped out and sure enough one of the trailer tires was chewed to bits.

We soon had the trailer jacked up. Cutter removed four lug nuts with no problem—but the fifth one turned round and round indicating a stripped thread. There was no way we could remove the flat tire, so we were stranded again. A few vehicles passed by, even a wrecker, none of which slowed down. Cutter tried his cell phone, but found the signal too weak.

I had visions of spending the night in my boat, while my crew trucked on home. Just then a dark green pickup pulled over and a young man jumped out and hollered, "What's the matter, Mister

Bob, you having trouble?" After explaining the problem, our friend (who turned out to be a friendly Fish and Wildlife officer I had met at JR's store) offered to drive to Monticello, Florida, get his cutting torch, drive back and cut the nut off. We didn't object and he headed off down the highway.

To make a long story shorter, he made it back in about an hour. It didn't take long to cut the lug bolt, and we were finally on our way again. The officer wouldn't take anything for his trouble, of course, but I quietly slipped the fish fillets into his truck.

I'm certainly not a superstitious man, but I must admit what day it was. You got it...Friday the 13th.

That was the bad, bad trip, showing that life usually balances off the good with the bad—or is it the bad with the good???

CHAPTER 13

Life Threatening Experiences

O Lord my God, I will give thanks to you forever.
Psalm 30:12b NRSV
For You have rescued my soul from death, my eyes from tears, my
feet from stumbling. Psalm 116:8 NASB

It is awkward to write about life threatening experiences. Being a survivor of several of these, I don't want to give the impression that I am favored in some way. Neither do I want to convey the idea that I have been good enough to deserve the deliverance I received. I do believe that I was spared by a gracious God for reasons I don't completely understand. Perhaps He has other tasks He wishes me to perform.

Late one afternoon after a great quail hunt, I was driving home with my two guests. It was still broad daylight and the winter sky was blue and clear. We were laughing and joking about the birds we had missed when a large truck passed us, pulling ahead about a hundred yards. Since I was driving, I was the first to notice. It looked like a piece of white cardboard floating in the air above and ahead of us. I paid little attention even though it seemed to be drifting our way.

The noise was like a cannon blast and shook the whole truck. The steel column on the left side of the windshield crumpled and ended up looking like a crooked elbow. It was then that it dawned on us that the white object was a brick, apparently picked up by the truck's tires and hurled high into the sky in front of us. The combined speed of the brick and our truck was probably 120 miles per hour. That steel column had saved our lives, for if the brick had come down a few inches further over, it would have penetrated the windshield and crashed into our bodies. I have thanked God for those few inches ever since.

A few years before, I was returning home from a fishing trip. My son Charles was driving while I was in the front seat beside him. We were on a two-lane highway and approaching a steep hill. Just as we reached the top, a car loomed up in our lane. The driver had passed another vehicle on a hill, absolutely blind. No one had a split second to think, but thankfully the guilty driver turned sharply off the road and went down a steep bank, thus avoiding a head-on collision. It was as close as you could come to a horribly fatal accident. It all happened in two or three seconds and was over, with Charles and myself thankfully still headed home, safe and sound. Charles stated that he saw the other car in his rear view mirror. It came to rest at the bottom of the grade with no apparent damage.

When we arrived home about ten minutes later, I began to wonder how that other driver would ever get back on the highway. Finally I suggested to Charles that we should go back and offer some assistance, which we did. The occupants were a young boy and girl, still scared witless. There was no way they could get back up the bank. Charles had brought his "come along"(a hand operated winch) and with his strength he jacked the car up the hill and back onto the highway. The couple were so scared, they never even thanked us. Come to think of it, we never thanked them for taking that big risk to avoid the collision.

Many years before this when I was just getting a start in the lumber business, my father and I, with two other foresters, were riding over a piece of timberland. We were looking at the marked trees. The weather was very hot, so we had the windows rolled up with the air conditioner whirring. That's why, when we went over a steep grade, we didn't hear the train coming. Just as we left the tracks a fast moving freight train almost took a coat of paint off our rear bumper. One or two seconds later and we would have been smashed to bits.

I have often thought of these experiences and thanked God for delivering me, for allowing me to continue my journey. It has also come to mind— not to pass up any opportunity He gives me to serve Him.

Just as we left the tracks a fast moving freight train almost took a coat of paint off our rear bumper

Part Four

CHRISTIAN VALUES IN CULTURE CONFLICT...

In America culture warfare is waged relentlessly. Secular materialism is battling our Judeo-Christian heritage with a ferocity that most people are unaware of. The individual Christian is at great risk as he or she is deluged each day by these great waves of consumerism and enticement. How can the Christian fight back?

CHAPTER 14

This Present Age

Do not be conformed to this world, but be transformed by the renewing of your minds, so that you may discern what is the will of God—what is good and acceptable and perfect. Romans 12:2 NRSV
See to it that no one takes you captive through philosophy and empty deceit, according to human tradition, according to the elemental spirits of the universe, and not according to Christ. Col.2:8 NRSV
Finally, brethren, whatever is true, whatever is honorable, whatever is just, whatever is pure, whatever is lovely, whatever is gracious, if there is any excellence, if there is anything worthy of praise, think about these things. Phil.4:8 RSV

On my journey toward faith, I experienced a continuing conflict with the values of our culture. In America today and in much of the Western World historic culture is under severe attack by secular materialism. Is it any wonder that many wilt under the blast of luxury cars, cure-all prescription drugs and sex to fill our lives with blissful pleasure? For the Christian it is a fight against the world, the flesh and the devil.

This secular attack upon American culture didn't just happen. A number of shock waves rocked the culture beginning in 1948. That year the first Kinsey Report unleashed what the news media called the "new morality." Although that report dealt with the break down of morality in human sexuality, the message of undisciplined behavior began to extend to other areas of life. In the mid-sixties a number of academicians and theologians proclaimed a "God is dead" theology. Even though this movement lasted only a short time, it contributed to the further secularization of our society. Court decisions crippled the community's right to curb pornography. For the first time a popular magazine, "Playboy" followed by "Penthouse" exhibited nudity and exalted sexual titillation.

The Vietnam War brought bitter divisions, massive protests, and serious questionings of the authority and integrity of our country's leaders. It was also the only war in which the United States was eventually defeated. Watergate and the President's resignation kindled further cynical distrust of our leaders.

Following these shocks came the popularizing of illegal drugs. Then Hollywood began to probe into the use of these features in R rated movies. X rated skin flicks followed until the pornography and the illegal drug industry became very big business.

To make matters worse, an avant-garde journalistic bias against morality and almost every semblance of Judeo-Christian history or values sprang up. Large, well-heeled organizations began to attack all signs of Christian symbols and influences. Prayer was prohibited in public schools. Concurrence of the American judicial system tended to codify and establish this trend. Christian clergy and believers were often depicted on TV as hypocritical, narrow minded, or at best comical imbeciles. All of this was done under the guise of "separation of church and state," protection of first amendment rights, and "freeing" people from traditional moral disciplines.

Today secular humanists can claim a number of victories. They have given us freedom to do anything that feels good, to avoid every moral discipline, and to disobey any authority with which we happen to disagree. They have given us freedom to vulgarize the language and freedom *from* acknowledging God in all public institutions and functions.

This perverted kind of freedom quickly transforms itself into license, self-discipline into self-gratification and faith into sampling every "new" and fashionable doctrine that comes down the pike. It has changed time-proven values into situational ethics and put the emphasis on *me* and *mine*. Is it any wonder that corruption is found at the highest levels of business and government?

Opposition to these trends in our culture is instantly attacked as being bigoted and prudish. Many times, religious leaders remain silent; they don't want to be held up to ridicule by the secular media.

Today there is also a great conflict among the cultures of the world. Some in the Islamic culture have called America the Great Satan, and while I don't endorse this in any way, I can understand where they are coming from. They see only the worst side of us, and they don't want our culture undermining and engulfing their own. They don't seem to understand that although we continually abuse the freedom we enjoy, that same freedom is worth fighting for.

Political freedom continues to be the greatest single value guiding and inspiring America. But freedom without faith and morality leads to questionable and uncertain ends. It is faith, which gives us values. Faith can endure without freedom even in the face of unbelievable persecution. I do not believe freedom can long endure without faith with its values and disciplines.

Faith encounters many obstacles in America today. And make no mistake about it, *we are engaged in a culture war for the souls of every man, woman and child in America.* I pray that we will someday understand what Jesus was talking about when he said, " and you will know the truth and the truth will make you free."[1] That's the freedom I long for, supported by the truth announced by Jesus at a synagogue in Nazareth. "The Spirit of the Lord is upon me, because he has anointed me to preach good news to the poor. He has sent me to proclaim release to the captives and recovering of sight to the blind, to set at liberty those who are oppressed, to proclaim the acceptable year of the Lord."[2] The truth was about God's love for us and His plan of redemption for all mankind.

Understanding this truth liberates us from the bonds of secular culture and arms us for all our struggles, using the same values and practices taught and demonstrated by Christ. Essential among these values are love, forgiveness, and good works.

[1]John 8:32 NRSV
[2]Luke 4:18,19 RSV

We took our shirts off and began to wave frantically.

CHAPTER 15

Jeopardy Makes Good Neighbors

Many spectacular scenes are witnessed when fishing on the open sea. God's creation becomes very evident and we are mindful of the beauty that surrounds us on every side. Spiraling cloud formations are constantly changing, at times resembling mountains rising from the sea. At different depths the color of the water changes. Deep water has an almost purple hue, which we identify with large fish. Changes occur in minutes—from a flat, mirror like surface, perfectly reflecting clouds and sky—to turbulent, rolling waves topped by white caps.

There is another unusual feature about entering the open sea. Out of the sight of land, a certain detachment from our normal existence settles upon us. This detachment draws us into a close kinship with other seafaring folks, especially fishermen. On the sea everyone is your neighbor. I have never asked for help without readily receiving it. Likewise, all who are in trouble are my responsibility. It is akin to the good will that prevails at Christmas time, except that this feeling is timeless. Even every friendly greeting is cheerfully waved back.

I will never forget an incident which occurred during my offshore fishing days. One of my motor props spun out when we were 30 miles offshore with no other vessel in sight. Another half-mile and my other prop also spun out. It was late in the afternoon and I thought all boats had long since headed to shore. My crew and I, with great concern, were trying to figure out our next move, when we sighted a boat coming in our direction. Its path would have passed a good quarter mile away from us, so we took off our shirts and began to wave frantically. We were at the point of giving up when the boat turned our way, and soon three young men were shouting to us, asking if we needed help.

We replied that we really did, and without any hesitation they took our line, cleated it and started towing us toward shore. Well, talk about a long ride! Our boat was just as big as theirs and the progress was agonizingly slow. Three hours later we finally sighted land. Some might think that act was "above and beyond the call of duty." But it was only the neighborly practice of the "brotherhood" of deep-sea fishermen, and was not the only time I received such kind assistance.

Nor was it all one way. I have never passed a boat that appeared to be in trouble without offering the same kind of assistance, and I have pulled many of them to shore. (But I must say I never had the opportunity of pulling one 30 miles in one afternoon.) I have also picked up numbers of people from the sea.

My first experience in saving such "castaways" occurred on one of my first fishing trips offshore. A friend and I were trolling for Spanish mackerel about 12 miles out. I had never hooked a big fish on my own boat. Suddenly I got a hard strike. The fish made two long runs, taking out line before I gained control. But out of the corner of my eye I noticed a boat dead in the water ahead of us. A large wave hit its transom and spilled into the cockpit, sending its back-end down until only the bow was showing. Three of the four fishermen had life jackets on while the fourth grabbed the protruding bow and held on for dear life.

All this occurred in just three or four seconds while I was still fighting my fish. My partner hollered for me to forget the fish and save the crew. But my mackerel was very large and would be the first big catch of my vessel. I quickly surveyed the floundering crew in the water and decided they could hold on a little longer. My fish was then quickly gaffed and we went to the rescue.

We pulled all four men on board with no real trouble, except that my boat would not hold six heavy adults. We were in danger of capsizing, so I slowly headed out to a large party boat in the distance. We were fortunate to reach it intact and transfer our wet and dazed guests.

I believe it could be said that we were *neighbors* to the four survivors, even if my reaction was slightly delayed. And isn't it a shame that we can't see all of life in the same light? Each day we are all in jeopardy of the force of Evil, Satan, and other forces of peril and danger. Why can't we change our course long enough to help each other out and score a few victories in the culture conflict?

CHAPTER 16

Love Thy Neighbor

" ...Who is my neighbor?"
Jesus replied, "A man was going down from Jerusalem to Jericho,
and fell into the hands of robbers, who stripped, beat him, and went
away, leaving him half dead... A priest was going down that road,
and when he saw him, he passed by on the other side. So likewise a
Levite, when he came to the place and saw him, passed by on the
other side. But a (despised) Samaritan...bandaged his wounds...put
him on his own animal, brought him to an inn and took care of
him... Which of the three, do you think, was neighbor to the man
who fell into the hands of the robbers?"
Luke 10: 29b,30,31,32,33a,34b,36 NRSV, (my parenthesis)
"This is my commandment that you love one another as I have
loved you." (Jesus speaking to eleven of his disciples.)
John 15: 12 NRSV

Webster's Unabridged Dictionary gives the meaning of *tolerance* as follows: a fair, objective, and permissive attitude toward those whose opinions, practices, race, religion, nationality, etc., differ from one's own; freedom from bigotry. At first glance *tolerance* appears to be one of the greatest virtues. It is certainly proclaimed that way in our culture.

The word, *tolerance*, is apparently not found in most translations of the Bible. I looked it up in Strong's Exhaustive Concordance and the closest word I found was *tolerable*, which is used only in a negative sense. Tolerance is found one time only in

74

two modern translations and here it is a substitute word for forbearance.

I then turned to St. Paul's writing on Christian virtues, which is summarized in what he calls the "fruit of the Spirit." Those virtues are love, joy, peace, patience, kindness, generosity, faithfulness, gentleness, and self-control.

In Jesus' Sermon on the Mount, He blesses all those who show forth certain virtues. They include: the poor in spirit, those who mourn, the meek, those who hunger and thirst for righteousness, the merciful, the pure in heart, and the peacemakers. Nowhere do we see those who are tolerant.

In the wilderness of the Sinai Peninsula God proclaimed, "You shall have no other gods before me... for I, the Lord your God, am a jealous God..."[1] There was to be no tolerance for the *practices* of those who worshipped other gods. There was to be no *permissive attitude toward those practices.*

Where does that leave us in regard to race and national origin? The Bible substitutes a better virtue—love. We are to love our neighbors as ourselves. And Jesus made it plain that neighbors include all, especially those of other races or religions. The word, *love*, in the Biblical sense applies to persons, not to what they might practice. Jesus even took it a step further. " But I say to you, love your enemies and pray for those who persecute you."[2]

What the world needs now is love sweet love. That's the title of a song popular about 30 years ago. Unfortunately the word, *love*, has been defined for us today by TV and other popular media. The primary meaning has become that emotion associated with erotic or sexual attraction, which may or may not be a part of what love really means. Sexual pleasure in itself can be very selfish, resulting primarily in self-gratification. In marriage, on the other hand, it can be the giving of one's self for the mutual gratification of both partners within the framework of absolute fidelity. Jesus endorsed this love at the marriage feast at Cana, where he worked his first miracle.

The Bible condemns fornication, a sexual experience outside of marriage essentially for hedonistic pleasure. Today's culture speaks of it lightly, even with titillation, euphemizing it into "sleeping with" or "having an affair with," and also "living with" or "hooking up with." Several popular magazines virtually advocate it. The Bible, of course, also condemns adultery, a practice, which if not outwardly condoned, is taken lightly by our culture.

Agape, that love which Jesus speaks about, always involves an element of sacrifice for the good of someone else. He said, "Greater love has no man than this, that a man lay down his life for his friends."[3] Paul in his famous 13th Chapter of 1st Corinthians defines love. His first two adjectives are *patient* and *kind*. He also says that love is not *self-seeking*. It is not boastful, arrogant, or rude. That eliminates pride, the root of most sin. Finally love endures without limit and is the greatest of all virtues.

Whenever love does not predominate in a church family, trouble is just ahead. I found myself in such a situation in my Episcopal parish a number of years ago. Our national church had made a major revision of the Book of Common Prayer, which was unacceptable to a substantial group of our members. This occurred about the same time that the renewal movement of the 1960s was beginning to influence many churches in America. The combination of prayer book revision and renewal practices resulted in a definite split in our congregation.

The more traditional group pulled out and established a new Episcopal parish. Looking back on that situation brings back many haunting memories. There was no right or wrong. There were two groups, each determined to dominate, making wholeness impossible. St. Paul in 1st Corinthians, chapter twelve, compares the church to a human body. Every part is important and necessary for its proper functioning. "If the foot would say, ' I am not a hand, I do not belong to the body,' that would not make it any less a part of the body." [4] The body thrives on the diversity of its parts. The church should also. What was missing in our parish?

The next chapter of 1st Corinthians, is all about *love*; it follows Paul's remarks about the church as a body. At first glance this chapter seems to be out of place until the relationship becomes clear. Without love, no direction or action of the church or its members will succeed. Love must prevail over everything else. That failure in our congregation separated families and life long friends into two different parishes.

Today, the wounds of that separation have largely healed. The parishes cooperate on a number of fronts and there is a warm feeling of being related in a special sort of way. Why? *Love* has worked its way back into the minds and hearts of the people.

The Supreme Court decision banning segregation in public schools provided a challenging opportunity to practice Christian love. I witnessed many examples of such love in my community on the part of both blacks and whites. Consequently, change in our school system took place peacefully, and if anything race relations actually improved. An urban renewal project provided the land, and a new public high school was built. A public golf course was constructed, giving all races a place to play golf. Leading civic clubs broke down the barrier against black membership, and our city commission immediately supported the public accommodations decision.

The recent decision of the Episcopal Church USA on acknowleging the blessing of same sex unions has brought a discordant note to that church body and indeed to Christians around the world. How are we to apply the principle of agape love to such a difficult question? There are apparently sincere Christians on both sides of the issue.

I know people who are homosexuals. Loving them with agape love and offering every ministry of the church to them should be no problem for Christians. Yet I do not believe Scripture teaching can bless this union, which would threaten the sanctity of marriage. In the grand human experiment, God created male and female and told them to be fruitful and fill the earth. Jesus, in answering a question by the Pharisees, proclaimed this same statement and added that a man should be joined to his wife so that the two become one.

Loving persons with an unqualified agape love and yet opposing their *practices* is not so difficult to grasp. In the early formation of the Christian church Peter and Paul clashed over how many Jewish practices should be essential for church membership. Yet I firmly believe they never ceased loving each other. I believe that the Holy Spirit will eventually lead the church to a conclusion consistent with the will of God on the polarizing question of human sexuality. I do not believe that schism within the Episcopal Church or in any other church body is the best answer.

How orthodox and evangelical Christians can effectively express their opposition to same-sex marriage within the greater framework of love in the Christian Community is one of the great issues of our day. Episcopalians are fortunate to belong to the world wide Anglican Communion, which is in the process of addressing this question.

There is no more important influence we can have on our culture today than to show the world what Christian love really is, and that *what the world needs now is love sweet love.*

[1]Deut. 5:7,9b NASB
[2]Matt. 5:44 NASB
[3]John 15:13 RSV
[4]1st Cor. 12:15 NRSV

CHAPTER 17

Forgiveness

"Forgive, and you will be forgiven." Luke 6:37b NRSV

Some of the principles taught by Jesus are very hard for Christians to understand and practice. I certainly count myself in that number when it comes to the principle of forgiveness. In fact, the virus of holding grudges seriously affected me until I was over 50 years old, and I cannot truthfully say that I am now completely cured.

There was a time in my life when I was struggling with a difficult spiritual problem. Somehow the message got through to me that I needed to forgive everyone who had ever hurt me.

Not knowing just how to accomplish such an impossible task, I simply drove into the deep woods and began to pray. In that prayer I asked God to forgive me for my lack of forgiveness. Immediately many images flashed upon my mind. People I thought I had forgotten came before me, and I sought forgiveness from God for holding an interminable grudge against them.

Soon I began to experience a great feeling of relief as if a gigantic burden or weight was removed from my shoulders. But it went much further than that. I felt a wondrous lightness as I was bathed in God's love. Tears of joy came into my eyes and I began crying, something grown men are never supposed to do. The sobs came in great waves and as they tapered off, another wave would begin all over again. I don't know how long this lasted, but I stopped resisting as each wave brought relief and joy that is difficult to describe.

That was an unforgettable experience concerning the past, people no longer in my life. But what about the present? My father lived to be ninety-two. But the remarkable thing about his life is that even though he had experienced serious illnesses including heart attack and cancer, he was physically and mentally active almost until the end. When he was in his early eighties, a friend asked him what he attributed his longevity to. Expecting to hear something about exercise or diet, his friend was surprised to hear him say, "A Christian teacher taught me early in life never to let the sun go down on my anger or on anyone who has a grudge against me."

Jesus put it emphatically. " But I say to you that if you are angry with a brother or sister, you will be liable to judgment...So when you are offering your gift at the altar, if you remember that your brother or sister has something against you, leave your gift there before the altar and go; first be reconciled to your brother or sister and then come and offer your gift."[1] I believe this exhortation probably applies even to receiving the sacrament of Holy Communion.

Christians repeat this principle every time the Lord's prayer is recited. "Forgive us our trespasses as we forgive those who trespass against us."

The principle is eternal. When Peter asked how many times he should forgive a brother or sister, Jesus replied, "up to seventy times seven"(or an infinite number).[2]

Even when the Lord was suffering terrible rejection and pain, being nailed to the cross, he cried out, "Father, forgive them; for they know not what they do."[3]

It is clear from the Gospel that forgiving others is a prerequisite for our receiving forgiveness from God. But there is another— a penitent and contrite heart. Jesus came to save sinners like you and like me. Confessing our sins to the Lord is an important part of the Christian life. We can do it directly or at more difficult times through a priest or minister. Confession and repentance are essential. They cleanse our consciences, lift the burden of guilt, and put us back into a right relationship with God.

Forgiveness — giving or receiving it is a fundamental and unique Christian principle. By practicing this virtue Christians can set an example for healing old and new wounds and give deep meaning to the expression, "The peace of the Lord be always with you."

[1]Matt. 5:22-24 NRSV
[2]Matt. 18:22b NASB (author's parenthesis)
[3]Luke 23:34 RSV

CHAPTER 18

Forgiving a "Heartless" Fishing Pal

Over thirty years ago St. George was an almost uninhabited island off the historic fishing village of Apalachicola, Florida. It stood in abject contrast to the present resort with its million dollar homes and high priced real estate. There was a country store that sold bread, milk and a small assortment of canned goods. There were also four or five small rental houses. The Plantation resort development was just a dream in someone's mind, and the bridge had only recently been completed.

I had heard about the fabulous red fishing and moored my 22-foot boat at a slip in Apalachicola. From there we would cross Apalachicola Bay to fish in Sikes Pass. The Pass is a channel cut through the width of the 21-mile long island so that ships out of Apalach can move directly into the Gulf without traversing the island. About half way through the channel the sides are lined with giant boulders extending as a jetty almost one hundred yards into the Gulf. The swift waters of the channel and the large rocks attract redfish in great numbers as fall comes on. The Pass affords reds a shortcut to the Apalachicola River as well as a welcomed respite to feed on baitfish, also attracted by the rocks.

Red fishing reaches its peak in the cool fall months, but so does the wind coming off cold fronts. During most of this season small craft warnings are out, sometimes increasing to gale force. I can remember crossing back to the mainland after a red fishing trip to face six-foot seas, which crashed over our windshield, leaving us standing in several inches of water.

That is precisely why a couple of my fishing buddies, Cutter and Wayne, talked me into pulling a jeep down to the island. We could then drive it on the beach to the Pass. It sounded like a good idea, so at the next opportunity we were on our way. We parked our truck at the store and piled our fishing gear into the Jeep. I will never forget driving past miles of beautiful sand dunes covered with sea oats and yucca. On that fall day the sky and water were a clear, translucent blue interrupted only by the white caps of the breaking waves, a perfect snapshot of God's majestic creation. There were no fancy three story homes lining the beach or any sign of civilization.

Arriving at the Pass, we grabbed our fishing gear and headed for the rocks. Climbing over the large boulders was no piece of cake. Good footholds were few, and sometimes we had to jump the spans between rocks. One misstep could result in a broken leg or an ugly gash. Wayne stopped first, then Cutter. I took the position at the end of the rocks. We fished for about two hours. I caught a good-sized speckled trout, but the fishing seemed very slow.

When I decided to wrap it up, I gathered up my gear and climbed back toward the others. Cutter had found a flat rock on the east side close to the water level. This had put him out of sight. When I came upon him, he was standing there looking like the cat that swallowed the canary. The fish string across his shoulders was

He was standing there, looking like the cat that swallowed the canary. The fish string across his shoulders was filled with five-pound redfish

literally filled with five-pound redfish. With that much weight, he couldn't climb the rocks.

I was shocked at his fabulous catch and even more at his failure to share the fishing with us. I even entertained the idea of leaving him to go it alone, but I relented and relieved him of half the load. We then made our way slowly and cautiously back to Wayne, who had caught nothing. He and I were greatly miffed at Cutter's secret honey hole, but decided to *forgive* him. After all, his great catch would provide us with some delicious repasts, and we both felt a tinge of admiration for his canny fishing ability.

We loaded the Jeep and headed back down the beach. It was then that I came up with a brilliant idea. Why not gut the fish right there in the shallow surf. Wayne volunteered to do the job in spite of the fact that he caught none of the fish. Cutter and I moved about seventy-five yards away from Wayne and began to surfcast. Wayne was standing in ankle deep water with his back toward the Gulf. He was gutting the fish and throwing the remains behind him into the surf.

After a few minutes I happened to glance Wayne's way, only he seemed to have some very strange company. A large black object appeared just behind him, almost at his heels. I quit fishing and walked back in his direction. As I drew closer, I couldn't believe my eyes. The black object was a large shark, straining on its side to stay in the shallow water while practically catching the discarded fish guts.

It reminded me of an entertainer throwing fish to a trained seal. Except this was a shark, and all it was trained to do was to eat everything in its path. I wanted to laugh at that strange panorama, but I realized that danger was lurking at Wayne's heels, so I shouted to get his attention. When he finally heard me and turned around, he jumped up and literally flew out of the water.

His source of food having disappeared, the big shark slowly turned and took off for deeper water. Saltwater sports are fun and exciting but can quickly turn dangerous. I have been greatly blessed that all my adventures have ended up on the lighter side.

Wayne seemed to have some very strange company.

CHAPTER 19

Works, Too, Are Necessary

But be doers of the word, and not merely hearers who deceive them-
selves. James 1:22 NRSV
Just as the Son of Man did not come to be served, but to serve...
Matt. 20:28a NASB

What is it that has made democracy work in America when it is so hard to establish and practice in other countries? It might be our great Constitution and our Bill of Rights. But model constitutions have been tried with little success in other countries. It might also be that faith in God, held by the great majority of our founding fathers, along with the place of God in our branches of government (which today is constantly threatened) share much of the credit.

I believe that one probable answer is the institutions we take for granted. The public schools, public libraries, community hospitals and medical centers, the United Way with its many participating organizations, our churches, YMCAs, Habitat for Humanity, Boy's and Girl's Clubs and on and on. Also the people who work for them, govern them, and fill the volunteer ranks without pay. These institutions might be the last bulwark in a culture faltering under the constant pressure of secular materialism. Our wholehearted support of them might help turn the tide.

Shortly after I came home from college, my pastor asked me to become chairman of a local charity board. In this country, if you are available and willing, there is no end of worthwhile institutions you can serve. In every case I found that I got far more out of the service than I put in. This willingness enabled me to participate in many exciting community activities, help to establish new ones, and even serve in an elective office.

Part of my drive came from a desire to follow my father, who had been a real community leader. But I must confess a less noble reason: I was very ambitious to become a maker and shaker in my community.

It is important for every able person to participate in these democratic institutions. In many instances they are the yeast that makes the dough rise, and the volunteer or elected official experiences a real sense of fulfillment. It is also an opportunity to sacrifice some of our time in service to others, even if a tinge of ambition is involved.

There are also opportunities to serve individuals, who are in need. Recently I was late arriving at church for an important meeting. As I entered the hall, a young man accosted me. I knew him from previous occasions. He evidently has a mental impairment of some kind and is quite often hanging around asking for help. I tried to avoid him, but he wouldn't let me. He asked for help, and in this case it might not have been money or food. I replied that I couldn't help him and rushed into the meeting. Later that evening, his pleading face came back into my thoughts. I should have stopped to offer assistance, and I asked the Lord to forgive me and give me another chance.

It might even be that the most important works we engage in are not institutional or even notable. From the time we arise in the morning and throughout the day we are confronted by people, problems and choices. The attitudes we display and the actions we take in dozens of common experiences constitute our "works." Remaining faithful in these small matters requires much dedication, humility, and presence of the Spirit.

Rendering community service and taking time to help those in need gives Christians an opportunity to fulfill Christ's answer to the following question. When did we see you thirsty, hungry, sick, or in prison and offer to help you? He answered, "Truly, I say to you, as you did it to one of the least of these my brethren, you did it to me."[1] Blessed indeed will be those who practice such deeds.

All Christians have been given the power to change lives through communicating the Gospel of Christ. This too is an important part of our works. Some have the gift of evangelism—person to person. Others have the gift of teaching, preaching, writing or witnessing. Whatever the method being employed, Christians *must* carry the Gospel out into the community and to the world. Such is our call and commission.

¹Matt. 25:40b RSV

Part Five

GOOD NEWS...

I have a friend who always greets me with, "I have some good news." There's nothing like good news to raise our spirits and put a smile on our faces. Good news about fishing is greeted eagerly by every angler, while good news from God is necessary for our salvation.

CHAPTER 20

Good News Bass

The striped bass is one of the great game fish of the Eastern Seaboard. The beaches near Cape Hatteras in North Carolina and the Chesapeake Bay are favorite haunts of this large fish, which also inhabits the waters of the Gulf of Mexico but in lesser numbers. In fact, South Georgia and Florida are on the borderline of the population since it prefers cooler waters.

The striper was considered a salt-water fish even though it ran far up the rivers to white or swift water during the spawning season (its eggs must be laid in swift water.) Then an unforeseen thing happened. In South Carolina some waterways were dammed up, creating the Santee-Cooper Reservoir. It so happened that large numbers of stripers were trapped, cut off from the sea, and became residents of the fresh water compound. These fish flourished, proving that stripers can live comfortably in either salt or freshwater. The sportfishing community eagerly took to fishing for fresh-water stripers, primarily because of their large size and great fighting ability.

This thrilling sport, however, was not enjoyed in the rivers and reservoirs of South Georgia and Florida because of the striper's preference for cooler water. There was a fish that did well in these waters—the white bass, but its size was puny compared to the striper. That presented a challenge to state biologists. Happily, they were up to solving the problem by crossing the white bass with the striper. I believe Florida succeeded first and began stocking the fresh waters of that state with fingerling hybrid bass, which they called Sunshine Bass. Georgia was soon to follow with a program of its own, which successfully crossed the two fish.

The result was *good news* for fishermen — a fish that would grow to almost 20 pounds in North Georgia and to 9 pounds in South Georgia and Florida.[1] Its appearance was similar to a striper except the stripes were uneven, not lined up perfectly from head to tail. Also its shape was stockier and not as long as the striper. But its game quality was equal to the striper. One columnist described its action as that of hooking onto a fast moving freight train. Naturally such a description captured my interest, although I was predominantly a saltwater fisherman.

The greatest problem with the hybrid bass is its inability to reproduce itself. Consequently it has to be stocked by the states each year. State hatcheries produce thousands of fingerlings, which are stocked in many waterways.

The Chattahoochee River dividing Georgia and Alabama, together with its various reservoirs became prime stocking areas. The stocked area closest to Thomasville, Georgia, is Lake Seminole, formed by the confluence of the Chattahoochee and Flint rivers with Spring Creek. Good spots are also found further north below the George W. Andrews Dam at Columbia, Alabama, and the Walter F. George Dam at Fort Gaines, Georgia.

Hybrid bass feed upon threadfin shad, a small 3 to 4 inch fish. Catching shad is almost as challenging as catching the bass. I used a four-foot throw net, and at times a long handled bait net to scoop along the wall leading to the lock at Columbia. Even after I caught on to the sport, I was always at a disadvantage at Columbia because of the time it takes to make the trip. By the time I arrived, the fishing area below the dam was usually filled with boats.

The season at the dam sites begins in early spring "when the dogwood leaves are as big as a squirrel's ears" as the saying goes. This is the time when hybrid bass, thinking they can spawn as well as any other fish, swim upstream to white water released from the dam. This maneuver is strictly instinctive based on the striper genes in its makeup. The fish actually grows roe, which is good to eat but absolutely sterile.

One of the best spots to fish is the discharge from the atomic energy plant south of the Columbia dam. This plant uses river water to cool the reactors. When the water is released back into the river, it is still warm and gushes out of a narrow channel, attracting shad, which in turn attract hybrids. We normally anchor so that we can cast shad lures into the white water flowing from the plant and "drown" live shad on the bottom behind the boat. I have hooked as many as six hybrids in six casts into the swift white water. The fish dart back into the river and put up their usual thrilling fight. In the meanwhile larger hybrids feeding on the bottom occasionally strike the bottom rigs.

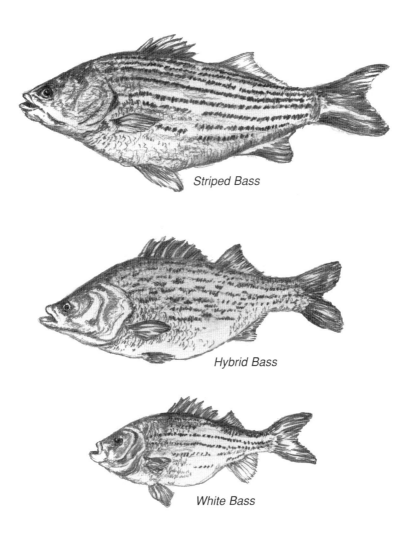

Striped Bass

Hybrid Bass

White Bass

One of my best trips to the dam site occurred one Thomasville Rose Show day. My friend and fishing pal, James Day and I headed for Columbia early that morning. We got there soon enough to catch bait schooling along the lock wall and were fortunate to find an empty spot in the swift water pouring out one side of the dam. Getting the boat securely tied up in that fast moving water is tricky, but we managed to tie on to one of the buoys holding a wire cable. This device keeps fishermen at a safe distance from the more turbulent waters flowing from the dam. We each baited up with live shad and let the lead sinkers take them to the bottom.

What followed was better than a three-ring circus. A large school of hybrids was feeding almost under our boat. We would get a strike on one rod, and before we could land the hard fighting fish, another rod would bend double. In less than thirty minutes we had two limits of hybrids in the box. It was exciting, but after that brief battle, we had nothing to do but head back to Thomasville on our long ride home.

Before we could dispatch a fish to the cooler, both rods would be bent double.

That trip gave us a very false impression. The trips that followed were no slam-dunk. The shad were sometimes almost impossible to catch, and we never caught hybrids in another feeding frenzy. So we usually had to settle for two or three fish apiece at the very most.

As in most kinds of fishing, we discovered a new way to catch hybrids. One day when we arrived at the dam site it appeared that every good spot was taken. It was going to be difficult to catch shad with so many boats in the way. However, after completely disrupting and irritating several fishermen, we were able to put a few live shad into the bait well. I was hoping the atomic plant discharge was unoccupied, but upon arriving, we found the spot filled with three boats.

We were literally loaded for bear (hybrids) with no place to go. Necessity is the mother of invention, so I reasoned that some shad would be gathered wherever water was discharging swiftly into the river. I soon found a creek that matched this description. We anchored slightly above it so our bait would rest on the bottom just downstream of the creek. We sat back and waited for a half-hour with our rods in the rod holders.

Suddenly the tip of my rod bent quickly, then straightened up. Just as I grabbed the rod, the hybrid swallowed my shad. He took off downstream in a run that ripped yards of line off my reel. I wasn't sure I could hold him, but almost at the end of my line, he circled, giving me several yards back. He was now in the center of the river doing pretty much as he pleased. The river current pulling against me didn't exactly help either. After being shown every possible kind of gyration, I slowly fought him toward the boat and my partner netted him. He was the largest bass I had ever caught, weighing just over nine pounds.

I baited my hook with another shad and we settled back down with our rods again in the holders. After a few minutes of rest and some good ole' boy stories, my partner's rod bent double. He also had a good fight, with his bass only slightly smaller than mine. We ended the morning with only three hybrids, certainly not high boat, but the average size of our fish was amazing. They pushed the upper weight limits of the species in our area and gave us the satisfaction of finding another way to catch the prized hybrid bass.

The home of the hybrids that run upstream to the Columbia dam is Lake Seminole. After the spring run to white water, the fish return to the Lake for most of the year. That opens the possibility of fishing for them in the Lake. Seminole is much closer to Thomasville than Columbia, so in recent years I have confined my hybrid fishing to the Lake in order to avoid the two and one-half hour trip.

A good friend, Tom Hale, took James and me on our initial trip to the Lake. He took us to the old channel of Spring Creek, now far out in the Lake. It is marked by rows of trees and stumps on two sides delineating the old creek bed. We fished close to where the old creek bed ends in the Lake. We were casting artificial lures and caught one large hybrid and a nice four-pound largemouth bass.

Next he showed us how to find the hybrids in the open waters of the Lake. He would putter along slowly, watching his fish finder. When he spotted a large school of threadfin shad, he would stop the boat. We then cast leaded spoons to the bottom of the Lake and jigged them up and down as we made the retrieve. This method yielded several nice bass and some great sport.

On a later trip he showed me how to troll for them. For this to work you have to know the good spots where bass usually feed. Otherwise, it's like looking for a needle in a haystack. This last method is the one I adopted for later trips. We use a bright-colored stubby lure with a large scoop in front that pulls the lure several feet under the surface. The bass gather to feed on underwater sand ridges that attract shad. I know of only two such hot spots in the Lake, the other one consisting of the old Spring Creek bed itself.

One morning Judge Lilly and I set out for the Lake. The judge had been one of my first fishing pals. He is a distinguished citizen of Thomasville, having served as its Mayor for many years and as Judge of the Superior Court, Southern Judicial Circuit of Georgia. We trolled one of the sand ridges for an hour with no luck, so we headed for the old Creek bed. We trolled just outside the old channel and then straight up the channel. Occasionally we would hit a school of bass and boat a nice one. When a big bass strikes a trolling lure, for a few seconds it's like hanging onto a large log until the log starts fighting back. Hang-ups are many times mistaken for bass strikes and visa-versa.

We had experienced about average luck when I decided to troll all the way up the Creek bed, which is about twenty feet deep. The weather was very clear with a moderate wind blowing. We were both a little weary from the early morning activities. Trolling slowly along with the motor humming almost put us both to sleep, when suddenly the judge got a good strike. He jumped up on the boat's forward platform to fight the fish. About that time I also hooked into a bass. I cut the motor and became very engaged in fighting my fish.

The forward motion of the boat aided by the wind was pushing us toward the side of the creek bed. I heard the judge holler, but I was in the final phases of boating my fish, which I did before turning around. There was no judge in the boat. I ran to the front, thinking I would see him treading water, but instead, he was apparently standing motionless in 20 feet of water. I couldn't imagine how he was staying afloat. (We don't wear life jackets and the judge is well under six feet tall.) He was just suspended there in deep water with a funny expression on his face.

I finally stammered, "What happened, judge?
"You threw me out of the x%x#$x boat."
"What the heck's holding you up?" I gasped.
"I'm hung on a cotton pickin' stump. Get me off."
He really was hanging by the back of his shirt on a stump. He appeared to be suspended since the stump was hidden behind him.

Well, I pulled him off the stump and into the boat. The main damage was a large hole through his shirt and a slight laceration where the knot had penetrated. I later thought about putting a bronze plaque on that stump to commemorate the judge's "suspension."

You might think the Captain was embarrassed, but he wasn't. It was neither the first nor the last time that, becoming engrossed in landing a fish, he would find his partner in the drink.

"I'm hung on a cotton pickin' stump. Get me off."

Creation of the hybrid bass was one of the major accomplishments of scientific fish breeding. For the large number of people who don't live close to saltwater and fish in freshwater, it was an almost miraculous feat. The fish has the striking instincts of the small white bass and a size closer to the striper. Its strength and fighting ability are now legendary—*good news* indeed for sport fishermen.

[1]The Florida Game and Fresh Water Fish Commission (In a bulletin entitled "Florida Striped Bass" by Forrest J. Ware) reports hybrids exceeding 15 pounds, but that has never been my experience.

CHAPTER 21

The Eternal Good News—
A Miraculous Gift from God

But Moses said to God, "If I come to the Israelites and say to them, 'The God of your ancestors has sent me to you,' and they ask me, 'What is his name?' what shall I say to them?" God said to Moses, "I AM WHO I AM." He said further, "Thus you shall say to the Israelites, 'I AM has sent me to you.'"
Exodus 3: 13,14 NRSV
I am the living bread that came down from heaven. Whoever eats of this bread will live forever...
I am the light of the world. Whoever follows me will never walk in darkness...
I am the good shepherd. The good shepherd lays down his life for the sheep.
I am the resurrection and the life. Those who believe in me, even though they die, will live...
I am the way, and the truth, and the life. No one comes to the Father, except through me.
Jesus speaking in John 6:51, John 8:12, John 10:11, John 11:25, John14:6, NRSV

He said to them, " But who do you say that I am? Simon Peter (the big fisherman) answered, "You are the Messiah, the Son of the living God." Matthew 16:15,16 NRSV, (my parenthesis)
For in him all the fullness of God was pleased to dwell, and through him God was pleased to reconcile to himself all things, whether on earth or in heaven by making peace through the blood of his cross. Col.1:19,20 NRSV
For God so loved the world, that He gave His only begotten Son, that whoever believes in Him shall not perish, but have eternal life. John 3:16 NASB

How do we know God, to whom we pray and on whom we depend for our salvation? Since the beginning of the human experiment, mankind has sensed the existence of the Creator, the One whose hand brought the universe into being and set its motion into majestic order. Every civilization has recognized man's limitations and his dependence on a person or force greater than himself. St. Paul would later on describe this natural sense: "Ever since the creation of the world his invisible nature, namely, his eternal power and deity, has been clearly perceived in the things that have been made."[1]

Some tribes and nations developed multiple gods. The Greek and Roman civilizations had well defined gods and goddesses, to whom they built temples and made offerings. But it was the people of Israel, a small, insignificant tribe and eventual nation, which came to know the God of creation. The central belief of the Israelites was summed up in one great statement or creed: "Hear, O Israel: The Lord our God is one Lord; and you shall love the Lord your God with all your heart, and with all your soul, and with all your might."[2]

The concept of one God was not always kept by the Israelites who, influenced by the culture around them, at times fell away and began to worship other gods. But faith in this one God never completely departed from Israel and has remained steadfast for thousands of years.

God chose to manifest himself to a particular man, Abraham, who felt God's call upon his life. He left his own country and traveled to a land where he perceived God was calling him. He even made a covenant with God in which God promised that Abraham's descendants would be as numerous as the stars in the sky and that they would possess the Promised Land. Abraham's part was his faith and belief in the Lord, which God reckoned as righteousness. Later on, God promised that Abraham would be the father of many nations, and his seed would become a blessing for all nations. God's manifestation to Abraham came in the form of visions, dreams, and directly spoken words.

Six hundred years later God manifested himself to another man, Moses, who was assigned the role of freeing the Israelites from their masters, the Egyptians. This manifestation first took place in the flame of a burning bush, which was not consumed. God spoke to Moses from the flame. After the Exodus, God's presence was revealed to the Israelites in a cloud by day and a pillar of fire by night. God spoke to Moses on Mt. Sinai. His manifestation was fire and smoke, which enveloped the top of the mountain. No one was allowed to directly witness this presence of God except Moses and Aaron.

When God spoke to Moses, he gave him the Ten Commandments and other aspects of the Law including the Creed cited above. God also gave an important commission to the Israelites: "Now therefore, if you will obey my voice and keep my covenant, you shall be my own possession among all peoples; for all the earth is mine, and you shall be to me a kingdom of priests and a holy nation."[3]

God spoke directly to Joshua and to some of the Judges of Israel, but after Israel opted for a king, the word of God was revealed chiefly through the Prophets of Israel beginning with Samuel, followed by Elijah and Elisha. God spoke both directly and by visions to the Prophets, who pronounced his words to the kings and the people. Later, from Isaiah starting in 740 BC to Malachi prophesying about 430 BC, God's word continued to be revealed by the Prophets of Israel.

There ensued a period of 400 years when God remained virtually silent. During this time, the Persian, Greek, and then the Roman Empire ruled the Mediterranean World. This silence was prelude to the greatest manifestation of God in his Son, Jesus Christ. Salvation history, dominated by God's direction to the people of Israel, was about to be expanded by the appearance of the Kingdom for the entire earth. "Repent, for the kingdom of heaven is at hand,"[4] were the first public words of Jesus.

This manifestation of God was like no other before it. "In the beginning was the Word, and the Word was with God, and the Word was God. He was in the beginning with God; all things were made through him, and without him was not anything made that was made. In him was life, and the life was the light of men. The light shines in the darkness, and the darkness has not overcome it...The true light that enlightens every man was coming into the world."[5]

There was no question in John's mind that Jesus is of one substance with God. "He is the image of the invisible God,"[6] according to Paul. The coming of Jesus changed the world to the extent that all previous history was designated as BC (Before Christ) and all that followed as AD (in the year of our Lord).

I've often wondered how it would have been to live outside or "...alienated from the commonwealth of Israel, and strangers to the covenants of promise, having no hope and without God in the world."[7] However, this was the condition of most of the world before Jesus came. I wonder what my temptations and sins would have been without a sure knowledge of God. Paul has a description of those times and people. And although they should have sensed God by the created world and universe, "...they became futile in their thinking and their senseless minds were darkened. Claiming to be wise, they became fools, and exchanged the glory of the immortal God for images resembling mortal man or birds or animals or reptiles. Therefore God gave them up in the lusts of their hearts to impurity, to the dishonoring of their bodies among themselves..."[8]

The prophet Isaiah foreseeing the coming of Jesus proclaimed, "The people that walked in darkness have seen a great light; they that dwell in the land of the shadow of death, upon them hath the light shined."[9] I do not understand how we in the church can fail to be constantly excited about the great salvation God has given us, the light that has shined for all to see, the wondrous love He has demonstrated to us.

Most people accept the historical fact that Jesus was a great man, whose revolutionary preaching changed the course of history. A good many accept the fact that he never wavered in his convictions and died a martyr's death, and that the principles he taught form the basis for mankind's moral values and laws. But what precisely is the real good news?

The previous manifestations of God had most often been marked by power and purity so great that humans could not come face to face with the Creator. He appeared in the fire and smoke and most humans could not draw near. There was a room in the Tabernacle and later in the Temple that was called the Holy of

Holies—the place where God met the High Priest of the Jewish nation once a year. No one else could even enter. This room was separated by a curtain, which we are told, was rent in two when Jesus died. The separation of God from man was literally torn down by Jesus. *Good news!*

The holy and invisible God had come to the earth in his Son, Jesus. He had been born of a woman and had become a man, who walked the earth, taught the eternal truth to men and women, loved with divine love, experienced the anguish of the human soul, and suffered and died for our sins. He came very close to us. He closed the gap, which had existed since the beginning. He could be touched and even embraced. *Good news!*

He did not come as a ruler, but as a carpenter. In his ministry his role was that of an itinerant teacher or rabbi.

When he took our place on the cross, he paid the price for our sins. Following the Law, the Hebrew had always made animal sacrifices to God. They believed there could be no forgiveness without the shedding of blood. The most important sacrifice was the shedding of an unblemished animal's blood to take away the sins of the people. This sacrifice was made year after year, the repetition showing that it was never complete. "And it is by God's will that we have been sanctified through the offering of the body of Jesus Christ once for all...For by a single offering he has perfected for all time those who are sanctified."[10] When Jesus, who was without sin, went to the cross he took upon himself the sins of all people for all time. His sacrifice eliminated the need for further animal sacrifices and he became the true Lamb of God who takes away the sins of the world. Our sins can now be forgiven through confession and repentance, lifting our burden of guilt. *Good news!*

On the third day he rose from the dead and appeared numerous times to his disciples before returning to his Father. *Good news!*

Before the Son of God was crucified, He promised to pray to the Father to send the Holy Spirit to his faithful; to strengthen, encourage, teach and empower them for ministry. This manifestation of God came upon the disciples at Pentecost, as tongues of fire appeared over each head and the sound of a mighty wind swept through the house.

Simple fishermen and artisans were transformed from a terrified flock in hiding to a strong band of evangelists, willing and able to carry the *good news* of Christ to the whole world. They lost their fear of the religious authorities and the Romans, and people in Jerusalem from many nations understood their words. They went out literally to turn the culture of the world upside down!

The same Spirit is present today. All baptized Christians have been given this wonderful gift. *Good news!* But we have to believe and accept the Spirit until we are filled to overflowing. He will not force himself on anyone. Are we up to the task of turning our present culture upside down?

Jesus came to save us from our human frailties, our sins. He destroyed the work and power of Evil when he rose from the grave. *He has promised eternal life to all who accept his words and believe in the Father.* "Truly, truly, I say to you, he who hears my word and believes him who sent me, *has eternal life*, he does not come into judgment, but *has passed from death to life.*" [11] Eternal life is ours, now! We don't have to wait until we pass from this world.[12] Too good to be true? But it is true. It is his gift of love to us. It is the *wonderful good news* of the Gospel.

On the third day, he rose from the dead and appeared numerous times to his disciples before returning to his Father.

105

I have often thought that no one could even imagine such a gift, such *good news*. Only God could come up with that plan of salvation. This is the God I know and trust and love.

[1]Romans 1:20a RSV
[2]Deut. 6:4,5 RSV
[3]Exodus 19:5, 6a RSV
[4]Mattt. 4:17b RSV
[5]John 1:1-5,9 RSV
[6]Col. 1:15a RSV
[7]Eph. 2:12b RSV
[8]Rom. 1:21b,22,24 RSV
[9]Isa. 9:2 KJV
[10]Heb. 10:10,14 NRSV
[11]John 5:24 RSV
[12]*Cf.* Col. 2:12-13; 3:1-4; Eph. 2:4-7 RSV

Part Six

PERSEVERANCE...

Perseverance really pays off in fishing. The best fishermen wage patience and perseverance to bring home a good catch. The Bible tells us that to be saved, we must persevere to the very end.

CHAPTER 22

The Tough Go Fishing

Deep-water fishing has a fascination that is hard to match. You never know what you are going to see or hang into. The weather can be tricky and flirtatious at times, but the colors of the water and sky are never forgotten even years later. Back in the years before loran, a boat captain had to go mostly on dead reckoning. Of course, he had a compass and a chart, indicating readings to various spots and objects, but success depended more on experience and instinct than on electronic gadgets. Being a romantic, I somehow yearn for those days again.

We were in the midst of "those days" when my friend, James Day, told me his brother, Jesse, was retiring from the Air Force. At that time I was still fishing offshore, so Jesse asked to go on one of our deep-sea trips. That delighted me of course. Any excuse would do, but this was an extra good one. In "those days" James and I would leave the Ochlocknee River east channel and head 180 degrees. That would put us right on top of buoy 26, which was a little more than 10 miles offshore. We would then head 185 and run for almost an hour. Averaging about 23 miles per hour, that would put us about thirty miles offshore. Cutting the motors off, we would each put a live shiner on the bottom and let the wind drift us over a school of grouper or snapper. We repeated this routine successfully for more than a year.

In "those days" I owned a fast 22-foot fiberglass boat, which took the seas pretty well. Thirty miles out is a long way, and on the previous trip, James and I had encountered an unusual sight. The

Loop, a current similar to the Gulf Stream in the Atlantic, had evidently swung in close to shore, because when we reached the thirty mile point, we began seeing bill fish. Every once in a while a sailfish would jump. We even caught sight of larger fish, probably marlin, making a jump clear of the water. We tried trolling for them, but never got a strike. The sight alone, however, was one you'd never forget.

With Jesse on board, we headed out on our usual course. The weather was beautiful, very few clouds with a light west wind blowing. It was a day offshore fishermen dream about. We made it out to our fishing grounds in record time and began drifting our bait close to the bottom. The water was that beautiful rich blue with an average depth of 75 feet.

We were having a good time telling tales, laughing and joking, when James got a hard strike, which bent his large rod and put a strain on him. A few seconds later Jesse struck a good one and began a strenuous fight. Not wanting to drift beyond the hole, I ran forward to drop the anchor. I had done this dozens of times without incident, but on that day my foot caught the forward cleat and I fell hard on the deck.

I managed to shove the anchor overboard to clinch our spot, but something about my right hand didn't feel too good. Looking down I saw that one of my knuckles had almost dropped out of sight. When I tried to open and close my hand, I heard an awful grating sound. The realization that I had broken my right wrist dawned slowly on me, and then the pain came. But that old saying came back to me. "When the going gets tough, the tough go fishing." And that's exactly what I did.

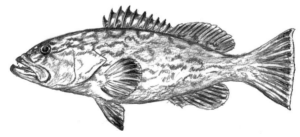

Gag Grouper

James and Jesse had both landed their fish, one being a medium-sized red snapper and the other a gag grouper going about 10 pounds. We obviously had hit a honey hole, and I wasn't going to let a little thing like a broken wrist keep the Captain from enjoying the action. I pulled out my handkerchief and tied it around my hand. (I didn't want the bone to stick through the skin.) I scarcely mentioned my problem, and we commenced to load the boat. Red grouper, gags and an occasional snapper were pulled aboard, all doing their best to stay on the bottom.

The maimed limb didn't hurt too much. All I had to do with my right hand was to turn the reel handle. My left did most of the work. We pretty well loaded our boxes and took a breather. James asked me if the wrist hurt. The Captain always has to be a "man" and I replied, "Not really." Although it was now beginning to ache.

Well, James relieved me from steering back to shore and everything went OK. When I reported to the Doc the next day, he couldn't believe I fished all day with a broken wrist. He just didn't know what hitting a honey hole thirty miles offshore is like. That type of *perseverance* was easy. In "those days" I'd gladly have done it again and again and...

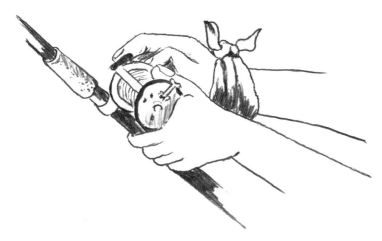

I pulled out my handkerchief and tied it around my hand.
(I didn't want the bone to stick through the skin.)

111

CHAPTER 23

Keep the Faith, Stay Alert, and Persevere

You must understand this, that in the last days distressing times will come. For people will be lovers of themselves, lovers of money, boasters, arrogant, abusive...treacherous, reckless, swollen with conceit, lovers of pleasure rather than lovers of God, holding to the outward form of godliness but denying its power. 2nd Timothy 3:1,2a,4,5 NRSV
But he who endures to the end will be saved. Matthew 24:13 RSV
And He who sits on the throne said, "Behold, I am making all things new." Rev. 21:5a NASB
"See, the home of God is among mortals. He will dwell with them as their God; they will be his people and God himself will be with them; he will wipe every tear from their eyes. Death will be no more...."Rev.21:3,4a NRSV.

What about the future? Are we to give it any real consideration? We make many secular plans for the future: our education, the education of our children, our vocations, our retirement, even next summer's vacation. Of course, Jesus tells us not to be anxious about it. Worrying will not change a thing. At my age and having had my share of illnesses, God has taught me to take life one day at a time, to do my best, to enjoy each pleasant moment, and to trust in Him.

Have you ever been concerned about God's plan for the future of mankind? Many have been and many books have been written about it. The Biblical books of Daniel and Revelation give us valuable clues about "latter days" on this earth. And remarkably similar accounts are found in the Prophets of Israel. They say it will be a day of gloom and darkness, of destruction and desolation in which all will recognize the great and holy God, who will bring vengeance upon all the disobedient. One thing is for sure: there will still be good guys and bad guys with the resulting conflict.

Daniel's vision predicts the first coming of the Messiah and even sets a probable timetable, which according to many has been very accurate. In interpreting Nebuchadnezzar's dream Daniel saw in a night vision the rise and fall of several world powers represented by portions of a great statue. But in the end he sees that a stone cut without hands will crush the great statue. The stone becomes a great mountain that fills the whole earth. The stone depicts God's Kingdom ruled by the Messiah.

A later vision describes what the end times will be like before the coming Kingdom. It will be "a time of great distress such as never occurred since there was a nation."[1] Only those found faithful to God and who endure until the end will be saved.

The fullest account of the last days is described in the book of Revelation. The story which follows is a highly abbreviated summary of Revelation.

Close to the end, the Antichrist will appear. He will gain political power by charisma and trickery until he is head of a worldwide government. Then the Antichrist will display his ruthlessness and utter wickedness until he sets himself up as god, requiring all people to worship him. Those who oppose him will not be allowed to buy or sell, making it impossible for them to survive.

Finally he will execute all who will not swear allegiance to him. Wrath will be poured out upon the earth in the form of terrible natural disasters. Faithful Jews and Christians will oppose the Antichrist to the end, which will see a great battle fought on the plain of Armageddon. The Lord will intervene and the Antichrist and his Prophet will be captured and sent into everlasting punishment. Thus the ultimate culture conflict will be resolved. The Messiah will reign for a thousand years on this earth. Later Satan, the manipulator of all evil will also be captured and sent into eternal punishment. God will change the old earth into a new earth, where

113

God and the Lamb will rule forever in the presence of the redeemed, living and resurrected.

From these two Biblical accounts, which basically agree with the Prophets, yet tell a much fuller story, it is evident that the end will be anything but peaceful. Of course the times we live in are also anything but peaceful. When I discussed this short scenario with my minister, he said, "I can give you a still shorter form. *In the end, God wins.*"

Jesus also gives an account of the last days in at least two places in scripture. In the parable of the weeds or tares, he tells of a man who sowed good seed in his field. While his men were sleeping, an enemy came and sowed tares. When both came up, his men asked him if he wanted the tares pulled up. But he told them not to do that since it might upset the wheat. His instructions were to let both mature, then gather the tares to be burned and the wheat to be put into the barn.

When the disciples asked the Master to explain the parable, he told them that He was the sower of the good seeds, which were the sons of the kingdom. The devil sowed the weeds, which were sons of the evil one. At the end of the age, the Lord sent forth his angels to gather together the evil ones, who were thrown into the furnace of fire. Then the righteous will shine forth as the sun in the kingdom of their Father.

Jesus' other reference to end times is in the conversation with the disciples on the Mount of Olives, called the Olivet Discourse.[2] He says that nation will rise against nation and there will be famines and earthquakes. He warns that many will hate his followers in those times. Many will be killed. Two of his statements are especially interesting: the gospel of the kingdom will be preached throughout the world and lawlessness will increase. Then he makes statements agreeing with the Prophets, Daniel, and Revelation: there will be a great tribulation such as the world has never seen. Also the sun will be darkened and the moon will not give any light.

Finally, the sign of the Son of Man will appear in the sky and he will come with power and glory and send his angels to gather together His elect from the four winds, from one end of the sky to the other.

The Biblical accounts written hundreds of years apart all essentially agree, and I guess the main message is: for Heaven's sake, be sure you are on the right side, now! Next week or next year might be too late.

Even I can see some of the prophesied events taking place and the reasonable possibility of others in the future. Israel has been gathered from the countries of the world to form a real nation again (a prophetic fulfillment). There is more lawlessness (Jesus, Olivet Discourse). There is an increase of knowledge (Daniel). The Gospel will be preached in all the world (Jesus, Olivet Discourse). Concerning the Antichrist's requirement that all people be marked with chips in their hands or foreheads to enable them to trade and do business, this technology has been developed.

Of course, the 64,000-dollar question is: when will all this take place? In answer to this, Jesus states that no one knows the day or the hour except the Father. What he does tell us in the Olivet Discourse is to be *alert*, watch, *be prepared, and in spite of every hardship, persevere to the end.*

[1]Daniel 12:1b NASB
[2]Matt. 24 and other Synoptics

EPILOGUE

I call heaven and earth to witness against you this day, that I have set before you life and death, blessing and curse; therefore choose life, that you and your descendants may live, loving the Lord your God... Deuteronomy 30:19,20a RSV (Moses speaking)
Rejoice in the Lord always; again I will say, Rejoice. Let all men know your forbearance. The Lord is at hand. Have no anxiety about anything, but in everything by prayer and supplication with thanksgiving let your requests be made known to God. And the peace of God, which passes all understanding, will keep your hearts and your minds in Christ Jesus. Philippians 4:4-7 RSV

Living in America as Christians in the 21st century is no easy task. On the international front we are engaged in a war against terror and on the home front we are mired in the culture war. Sometimes it's hard to tell which threat is the greater. As American casualties mount and we continue to offer democratic values to a divided Islamic people, we yearn for a successful consummation of the conflict in Iraq and Afghanistan.

On the home front the threat is much more subtle. It is the threat of derision and the threat of complacency. It is the threat of affluence, self-gratification and lust. It is the threat of an ever-increasing appetite for excitement—even violence. There is nothing new in these threats. They are great devices for turning Christian journeys into dead ends and denying us the abundant life promised by Christ. They have also been responsible for bringing down empires and civilizations.

Like many other Americans, I see and feel the advancing tide of evil and temptation. I am keenly aware of the culture war being waged for every human soul. I empathize with Paul when he says, " So I find it to be a law that when I want to do right, evil lies close at hand... Wretched man that I am. Who will deliver me from this body of death? Thanks be to God through Jesus Christ our Lord!"[1]

Nothing short of complete surrender to Christ will save us. Our wills, our pleasures, our ambitions, our lives must be overwhelmed by the Spirit of God. We must surely believe Jesus when He said, "I am the vine, you are the branches...apart from me you can do nothing."[2] We must plunge into the current of faith and swim with it, which will determine the direction of our lives forever. We will only then be able to resist temptation and begin to place the well being of others above our own. At that time we will be able to witness to the grace and power of God and see many lives changed and our own made more abundant.

And then, strange to modern, intellectual man, the current we become immersed in will begin to feel good, warm, internally welcomed. We will begin to feel that inner peace we yearn for. Our journey will be protected by blessed assurance. We will begin to experience the greatest joy a mortal is capable of. That joy, kindled in the heart will spread to our entire bodies and tingle our toes. The joy of fishing is one of my keenest pleasures. But the joy of the Lord is my strength *forever*.

[1]Rom. 7:21,24,25a RSV
[2]John 15:5 RSV

Bibliography

Hummel, Charles E. 1993. *Fire in the Fireplace, Charismatic Renewal in the Nineties.* Downers Grove, Illinois.

Gotthardt, Alan, 2003. *The Eternity Portfolio.* Wheaton, Illinois.

The Holy Bible, King James Version (cited KJV).

The Holy Bible, New American Standard Bible (cited NASB).

The Holy Bible, Revised Standard Version (cited RSV).

The Holy Bible, New Revised Standard Version (cited NRSV).